RELIGIOUS EDUCATION
IN THE EARLY YEARS

This volume looks at the role of Religious Education in the curriculum for the Early Years child. As this area of learning tends to be tailored to the needs of the local community, this book attempts to discuss a wide range of religious experiences and how these can best be enjoyed and explored to the full in an educational context.

Elizabeth Ashton's intention is to help readers clarify their thinking on the subject and she does so by looking at the development of some fascinating new approaches to the teaching of Religious Education.

Through studying practical examples and discussing good practice in the classroom, she provides a text that manages to be both inspirational and useful. This is a great addition to the Routledge series of books on Teaching and Learning in the First Three Years of School.

Elizabeth Ashton worked for many years as a class teacher in primary schools before becoming Lecturer in Religious and Moral Education at the University of Durham.

TEACHING AND LEARNING IN THE FIRST THREE YEARS OF SCHOOL
Series Editor *Joy Palmer*

The innovatory and up-to-date series is concerned specifically with curriculum practice in the first three years of school. Each book includes guidance on:

- subject content
- planning and organisation
- assessment and record-keeping
- in-service training

This practical advice is placed in the context of the National Curriculum and the latest theoretical work on how children learn at this age and what experiences they bring to their early years in the classroom.

Other books in the series:

GEOGRAPHY IN THE EARLY YEARS
Joy Palmer

HISTORY IN THE EARLY YEARS
Hilary Cooper

MATHEMATICS IN THE EARLY YEARS
Wendy Clemson and David Clemson

MUSIC IN THE EARLY YEARS
Aleuyn and Lesley Pugh

PHYSICAL EDUCATION IN THE EARLY YEARS
Pauline Wetton

SPECIAL EDUCATIONAL NEEDS IN THE EARLY YEARS
Ruth A. Wilson

RELIGIOUS EDUCATION IN THE EARLY YEARS

Elizabeth Ashton

London and New York

First published 2000 by Routledge
2 Park Square, Milton Park, Abingdon, Oxon, OX14 4RN

Simultaneously published in the USA and Canada by Routledge
270 Madison Ave, New York, NY 10016

Reprinted 2006 (twice)

Routledge is an imprint of the Taylor & Francis Group, an informa business

© 2000 Elizabeth Ashton

Typeset in Palatino by
M Rules, London

Printed and bound in Great Britain by
T J International Ltd, Padstow, Cornwall

British Library Cataloguing in Publication Data
A catalogue record for this book is available
from the British Library

Library of Congress Cataloging in Publication Data
A catalog record for this book has been requested

ISBN10: 0–415–18386–3
ISBN13: 978-0-415-18386-4

CONTENTS

BOXES

PREFACE

For many in education, both teachers and students, Religious Education is a controversial subject. It is neither a core nor a foundation subject: it is described as being 'part of the basic curriculum', and until 1988 it was the only subject that was required to be taught to all.

In the opening section of this book, discussion is developed with the purpose of helping readers clarify their thinking on Religious Education. This involves examining a few of the popular thinking movements which have exerted immense influence over the way in which popular opinion perceives religion, especially the apparent 'fact/belief' division and the way in which it has caused Religious Education to develop, particularly during the past few decades of this century.

The following sections of the book advocate an entirely new approach to the subject, one called evaluative Religious Education. This approach, by recognising the richness of the wisdom which is enshrined within the scriptures of the great world religions, sees religious insights as invaluable in that they offer people a yardstick against which life's experiences can be assessed and tested. It is shown, by means of many practical examples, how the ideas can be introduced to children in the early years of schooling.

The aim is not to condition children within any particular faith. The book sets out to examine conceptual development in Religious Education, and to show how closely religion is linked with language work and literacy, and the development of values.

As the book was in its final stages, the author read an account in a national newspaper of one of her former pupils. As a six year old, Michelle had loved History, Religious Education and English. However, she had never been motivated by Mathematics and the Sciences. As she progressed through primary school her early promise was not fulfilled, and she began to lose interest even in those subjects that had fascinated her at an early age. She did not co-operate in the secondary phase of schooling, as she came to believe that 'school is a waste of time'. She never passed any examinations and by the age of sixteen she had become a drug addict.

The newspaper account announced she had just been arrested and accused of the murder of a young man in an inner-city public house.

What values had Michelle's schooling encouraged her to develop? Her life at home was one thing, and as she herself made quite clear, her school life was quite distinct from it, and irrelevant. Yet school ought to be helping pupils to think clearly for themselves, and to distinguish between the good and the bad, the right and the wrong, and to acquire the ability of being able to predict cause and effect.

If this book helps teachers to see the role of Religious Education in a new way, one which could help the Michelles of this world avoid personal disaster, the purpose of the author will have been achieved.

ACKNOWLEDGEMENTS

I should like to thank the many students who gave permission for me to use several of their ideas in the practical parts of the book, and for their helpful comments and discussions.

On a personal note I should like to express my gratitude to Brenda Watson, whose friendship has been so inspiring – it changed the course of my career! I thank her for her generosity, especially for reading the script and making invaluable comments.

Again, on a personal note I should like to thank Miss Joan M. Kenworthy (formerly Principal of St Mary's College, University of Durham), who encouraged me to continue writing this book after I received news concerning my health which was, at the time, devastating.

My warmest thanks to all of these people.

Part I

WHAT IS RELIGIOUS EDUCATION?

The fact that Religious Education forms part of the basic curriculum for schools is, for many people, surprising. Some equate religious with social conditioning and argue that it has no place in the work of schools, whilst others believe religion in education ought to be about nurturing pupils within a particular religious belief system. People of both persuasions are likely to agree with the assumption that religion is about 'belief' whilst, for example, mathematics and science are about 'facts', although the majority of scientists and mathematicians would not agree!

The purpose of the opening section of the book is to open up the discussion of such opinions and assumptions, and the implications of the findings for the delivery of the subject among Early Years pupils. Three basic objections to Religious Education are identified in the opening chapter with the purpose of clarifying what the subject is really concerned to do.

The second chapter continues by looking at the real, educational purposes of religion in education. It begins by examining definitions of 'education'. This discussion is developed by then considering the specific function of 'religion' in education, leading to some lengthy consideration of the classical five-fold aspects of respect which lie at the heart of the great world religions, as can be understood when studying the truth claims of these belief systems.

The various approaches to Religious Education which have developed, largely as a result of assumptions discussed in the opening chapter, are discussed before a new method is advocated – conceptual development in religion, which recognises the importance of the individuality of each child in the school. Examples of this 'individuality' are given, although readers will undoubtedly feel stirred to apply the discussion developed to their own pupils.

1

CUTTING AWAY THE UNDERGROWTH

Misconceptions of Religious Education

Introduction

It is in their Early Years in school that many children can first be provided with opportunities to embark on a great voyage of discovery into the human search for understanding of the possible nature of life itself, including the non-material dimension. It is through study of the great religions of the world that pupils may be introduced to the great compendiums of wisdom which have been found, by many generations of people, to be supportive in times of stress, or when one is faced with the responsibility of making an important decision. However, there are a number of misconceptions of religion in the school curriculum which need to be cleared from the pathway of readers so that we can proceed to examine the real purposes behind retaining Religious Education as part of the basic curriculum in schools.

Three common objections to Religious Education are discussed in this opening chapter in order to clarify why the subject forms part of the basic curriculum of schools. The discussion will attempt to describe the common root system from which they have sprung.

Objection 1: Science is about facts; religion is just opinion

The search for totally reliable knowledge is, from a human perspective, entirely understandable. Which person in the world would not like to be certain that any disease which they suddenly developed, for example, could definitely be cured by modern medicine? However, as the vast majority of people who suffer serious diseases learn to understand, such certainty is just not possible. No matter how successful any treatment may have proved to be for others, there is no guarantee that similar success will be enjoyed by oneself, and of course, the opposite is true, too: one might survive against all the odds! This is because there are so many variables between individual circumstances, decisions made by the medical profession, and the extent to which the disease could have spread by the time of diagnosis.

This principle is true of all areas of life – it is by no means confined to medicine, and sadly there is a very difficult lesson to be learnt concerning the whole search for 'facts' (see, for example, Hawking [1993, 10] for discussion on the status of theories in physics). The lesson is that distinctions between supposed 'facts' and 'opinions' are not nearly as simple as was believed in the past, beyond the realm of empirically verifiable observations – for example, that there happens to be a cat sleeping on a particular hearth-rug, or that on 31 July 1998 the north-eastern region of England experienced very wet weather!

The assumption that a clear-cut distinction can be made between 'facts' and 'opinions' has its roots deeply embedded in the history of Western society. An associated notion, which has developed from it, assumes that alleged 'facts' are somehow more reliable than 'opinions', and that the study of the former is therefore a more worthwhile activity than the latter. It is not too large a step from this position to reach another, which is that anything that is unavailable for empirical verification must be doubted.

This easily develops into the assumption that morals, ethics and faith, for example, do not have 'factual' foundation; that they emerge simply from personal preference, or even from culturally conditioned choices. As an academic from an Asian background described the situation:

> In the West the dominant position is that of the philosopher A.J. Ayer. Essentially this is that moral judgements have no foundation beyond individual preference or cultural upbringing. In other words, you like or dislike something and that is the only reason for making any kind of ethical judgement.
>
> (Guptara, 1998, 30)

However, as Guptara goes on to explain, this view does not provide a basis for ethical issues because there exists a flaw in the reasoning on which the assumption depends. The flaw is underpinned by what are assumed to be two distinct types of evidence, outlined below:

1 *Empirical evidence* that has been gathered in as objective a manner as possible – that is, every attempt has been made to eliminate human opinion from the activity of data collection. This type of evidence is used in, for example, medicine and the study of the physical sciences. It is essentially physical evidence in that data are derived from the material world. Evidence of this type is, therefore, available for clinical analysis.

2 *Non-empirical evidence*, which is gathered and assimilated as a result of observations of phenomena that are not confined to the material realm

of life. Examples also include emotions such as jealousy, love, joy or anger. Because of the non-material nature of this type of evidence, it cannot claim to be objective, and is unavailable for clinical investigations of the type applicable to empirical evidence: one cannot do experiments with love or anger, for example, in the precise way that a histologist can distinguish cancerous cells from those that are normal.

Perhaps readers would find it helpful to spend a few moments reflecting on these two types of evidence, especially in relation to the following very important question.

- *Do you think it sensible, or misinformed, to consider evidence of type (1) to be of more importance than that of type (2)?*

Discussion

I believe that the most one could argue is that the two types of evidence are *different*. Type (1) evidence is available for empirical investigations, whilst type (2) clearly is not. However, this ought not lead to the assumption that evidence of type (2) is therefore inferior in some way to that characterised by type (1). Nor would it seem sensible to argue that emotions do not therefore exist! As readers are no doubt aware, human emotion in all its diversity is very powerful indeed and certainly exists. It is just that clinical analysis is inappropriate for non-material data: some other methodology is needed. Religion, of course, deals with phenomena that are more accurately described as type (2). It is interesting to note, nevertheless, that even data of type (1) must, in the final analysis, depend on human interpretation, so even that category of evidence can never be totally objective.

Unfortunately the history of Western society has encouraged more credence to be given to evidence of type (1) than type (2). The development of a movement known as *positivism* has been particularly influential here, in that it asserted that all claims to knowledge must be scientifically verifiable. Having its roots in the seventeenth century, the movement continues to be strongly influential today in most surprising ways – for example, many academics who would argue that positivism has run its course and has become superseded can frequently be found to be unknowingly thinking under its influence (see Chapter 3). This exemplifies the development of a movement known as metaphor in language! As a result, much energy has been expended in trying to make non-scientific disciplines, such as Education and Religions Education, scientifically respectable (see, for example, discussion on Depaepe, 1992, 67–93). Similar motivation has been influential in encouraging a movement in Religious Education called 'phenomenology'.

The question which must be faced, however, concerns *why* evidence of type (2) should be available, if it is to be deemed respectable, for scientific-type investigations. This question is, perhaps, all the more pertinent in the present climate of understanding which recognises that science cannot provide 'facts' of the type so confidentially heralded by nineteenth-century writers such as Auguste Comte (1969, 135). Would it not be more sensible to evaluate evidence of type (2) against a different set of criteria, since material pertaining to the two types are so fundamentally different?

The point may be illustrated further by a practical example drawn from the Early Years classroom. A student teacher told me how one of her pupils had asked if her grandmother (who had recently died) would come back to earth as something else, perhaps a horse of a dog. The student argued that she had terminated all discussion since it was not possible to give answers! This was a very sad conversation, but it did reveal misconceptions held by the student concerning Religious Education and was therefore helpful in providing a 'window' into her thoughts. What would be the likely effect of refusing to discuss with the child the Hindu doctrine of reincarnation? The message spelled out to her was clear: education only deals with knowledge of which we are certain. As we cannot be certain of the truth of religious doctrines, they are not worth studying!

No doubt most readers would indignantly repudiate such a view, and yet it does underlie very powerfully the 'Objection' which has led to the above discussion! It could be interesting to ask oneself how far such attitudes contribute to an initiation into secularism, rather than true education, characterised as it is by a spirit of free enquiry which is respectful of individual pupils. These points are developed further later, but especially in Chapter 6.

Objection 2: 'Religion is a personal matter, unlike science which is factual'

Elements of this objection are similar to those identified in the previous discussion – for example, that science is about 'facts' whilst religion is 'personal', that is non-factual. However, this objection goes further in that it implies that education ought not to interfere with what is apparently personal, but should concern itself only with what is deemed to be impersonal.

As might be obvious to readers, the assumption on which this notion rests is very precarious indeed! At least two objections could be raised against it:

1   Although one's relationship with one's God could, indeed, be deemed to be personal, the relationship itself will obviously bring into play a host of responsibilities that are of significance to wider society generally, rather than being confined to oneself. For example, religious faith

has serious implications for personal relationships, stewardships of the earth, attitudes towards wildlife generally, as well as for the quality of one's personal contributions to the life of both local and wider communities.

Also raised is the whole question surrounding education: what it is and what its purposes should be: for example, a life-long journey, rather than a series of skills and knowledge to be acquired. The journey of faith travelled in isolation from one's fellow creatures would be a lonely excursion indeed, as well as one artificially restricted. Experiences of religion tend to illuminate the impossibility of keeping one's insights to oneself. For example, St Guthlac (673/714 CE) left his monastery to take up life as a hermit at Welland, in remote fenland. What he discovered was that his privacy was invaded much more in his new home than it had been in the old, for all manner of people from far and near disturbed him, seeking his advice, such was his reputation for being the possessor of wisdom!

If Religious Education is understood as being about refining one's understanding of life itself through the insights gained by people of a particularly significant religious perception, it seems to follow that the wisdom derived from personal reflection should be available for succeeding generations, rather than remaining locked up in any individual's mind.

2   The second objection relates to another assumption implicit in the statement, that is, an uncritical acceptance of the apparent distinction between 'facts' and 'opinions', as discussed above. This is bolstered by a tendency to assume that only supposed 'facts' are legitimate for educational study! The error of this position can be illustrated in many ways, most practically perhaps by pointing out the context of education, which in the 1992 Schools Act is stated as being about pupils' 'spiritual, moral, social and cultural' development, just as it was under the terms of the Education Act of 1944. Religious Education has, quite clearly, a central role to play in these circumstances.

Objection 3: 'Schools are not the places to preach religion because it is impossible to determine whether it is true'

The presence of the 'fact–belief' division may by now be obvious to readers. However, this 'objection' embodies another, namely that education is confined to dealing with phenomena, or subjects, that are capable of being proved, rather than with those elements of life which could be false. The mistaken nature of the assertion is not difficult to illuminate; it is, in a sense, closely connected to the foregoing discussion under Objection 2. Most people will quickly recognise education in religion to be about testing insights and ideas, or about re-evaluating the insights of others in order to deepen one's own understanding of reality in its broadest sense. To assert that education is only about investigating what is already known (that is the 'factual') is simplistic and likely to be offensive to those who had an appetite for discovery, enquiry and invention.

Conclusion

The foregoing discussions have pointed towards a unifying element in all three assumptions which have been 'put under the microscope'. This element concerns the human search for what is sure and certain: a search that is ultimately doomed to failure if confined to such narrow limits. Any believe in a firm distinction between 'facts' and 'opinions' usually sees the former as being superior to the latter, rather than recognising the need for a different set of criteria for assessment.

Readers are now invited to spend some time examining any further objections they feel ought to be raised concerning Religions Education. It could be particularly helpful to analyse them according to the points made above, for most objections of this kind can be found to have originated in attitudes conditioned by positivism.

The following chapters of the book have been written in the belief that the great religions of the world offer criteria against which each individual can make an informed assessment of what happens in life, whether or not one agrees with the insights offered by religions or not. Because many religious teachings have passed 'the test of time' in that they have been found, throughout countless generations and across diverse cultures and regions of the world, to be sustaining in times of trouble and stress especially, it may be deemed that children are entitled to become aware of their existence as both a personal and cultural right.

The next chapter therefore turns to the question of what Religious Education is concerned with, now that we have dealt with what it is *not*. We should then be in a position to explore ways in which the subject may be approached in the classroom.

2

EDUCATION IN RELIGION

Introduction

The title of this chapter has been deliberately transposed: the reader might find it worthwhile to reflect on any differences between 'Education in Religion' and 'Religious Education'. Perhaps the most interesting is that it places 'education' before 'religion', possibly implying that it is education which is to lead the discussion, rather than religion. To put it another way: the chapter is concerned with how human experiences of religion can somehow be adopted for the purposes of education. This is quite a departure from past practice when the subject was called 'Religious Instruction'. The significance of the shift in emphasis might be worthy of reflection.

The intention of this chapter is two-fold. First, the plan is to discuss what the word 'education' might mean to different people. The definition adopted by the author will be offered to readers for their own assessment, in the hope that they may be persuaded to adopt it for themselves. Second, an investigation will be developed concerning how religion in education can be understood. The chapter will conclude by bringing the two terms together in order to define the role of Religious Education in the basic curriculum of schools.

What is 'education'?

This might appear to be a rather basic question, but it is not as simple as might first be thought. Box 2.1 offers readers various definitions of education, and it is proposed that an evaluation of each be made before continuing with the reading of this chapter.

Box 2.1 What is education?

1 The development of human potential
2 Learning to obey elders and betters
3 Indoctrination
4 The acquisition of skills and knowledge
5 Becoming familiar with the rules of society
6 Learning to respect beauty, truth, others, the environment and oneself
7 Development of the capacity to earn one's living

Discussion

The first definition of education ('The development of human potential') is frequently given and yet rarely criticised in spite of its vagueness and ambiguity. Whilst educators who favour it will no doubt understand 'potential' as relating to positive attributes of people, there is no guarantee that this is what 'education' usually achieves. The question that needs to be asked is whether it is wise to attempt to develop all human potential. The folly of any such attempt is not difficult to recognise. It is undoubtedly true that human beings have the potential for achieving a great number of enviable virtues, but sadly the reverse is also the case. Box 2.2 provides some of these polarities, with the intention of encouraging readers to recap on the lives of people about whom they have read (or perhaps others whom they know), and deciding whereabouts on the continuum that particular person could honestly be placed.

Box 2.2 Putting people on the line: human potential

LOVE . . . . HATRED
KINDNESS . . . . CRUELTY
HONESTY . . . . DISHONESTY
MODESTY . . . . CONCEIT
WISDOM . . . . FOLLY

It should be clear that educators need to make explicit which potential they are in the business of developing! This discussion might seem to be dealing with the obvious, or even flippant, and yet all too often education, through the hidden curriculum, can train children, albeit unwittingly, to develop negative potential, as has been discussed elsewhere (e.g. Watson and Ashton, 1995, 1–7).

A further example may be drawn from the author's personal experience of teaching, when a six year old child presented her with a beautiful bunch of daffodils. Innocent at that early stage in her career, the teacher praised the child for his kindness. It was only later in the staffroom that a colleague mentioned the donor of the daffodils had been spotted stealing the blooms from a neighbouring garden as he made his way to school that morning. I leave readers to reflect on what could have been appropriate action for the teacher!

There is a dangerous note of authoritarianism inherent in the second definition of education ('Learning to obey elders and betters') as there is in definition (5) ('Becoming familiar with the rules of society'). Both resemble remarkably some of the pronouncements made by Mr Brocklehurst to Jane Eyre (Watson and Ashton, 1995, 136–7). Children are remarkably resilient in the face of both dogmatism and authoritarianism, with the result that both are well known to be counter-productive in efforts really to educate. From the framework of this definition, education appears to be a means of social control, brought about by force. How far do readers accept this position, especially if education is understood as being a process of 'drawing out', of developing the capacity to think independently?

Regarding definition (3) ('Education as indoctrination') the word 'indoctrination' is itself very interesting, as pointed out by Watson (1987, 12–13). Whilst for some it is a word that can be substituted for 'teaching', for others it is exemplified by such twentieth-century movements as Nazism and Communism, characterised as they are by ideological manipulation. For others, to indoctrinate could imply attempts to condition the mind to accept certain dogmas in ways that stifle the investigation and questioning of them. It is this latter definition which is usually levelled against Religious Education, reflecting perhaps reactions to dogmatisms of times past.

Indoctrination thus understood takes on sinister overtones which are opposed to open enquiries into the whole spectrum of beliefs and values. It is therefore directly polarised to genuine education. Readers might like to reflect on this *vis-à-vis* subjects of the curriculum other than Religious Education: how much do science and mathematics, for example, run the risk of becoming indoctrinatory? Interestingly enough, charges of attempted indoctrination and conditioning are rarely levelled at subjects that are not obviously concerned with beliefs and values. The apparent distinction between objectivity and subjectivity is extremely plausible: the supposed difference between 'facts' and 'opinions' thus has far-reaching implications for views on arts subjects in particular (see Chapter 1 for a more detailed discussion). The proposition put to readers is that education understood as a journey of discovery towards truth, in its many dimensions, is the only safeguard *against* indoctrination, since it is based within methods of enquiry that must be free of all mental and emotional constrains and conditioning factors.

Turning now to the fourth definition of education ('The acquisition of skills and knowledge'), even a cursory glance at daily newspapers reveals how notions of education soon become narrowly equated with 'skills' and 'knowledge'. There are many dangers inherent in this perception, however, as evidenced in Box 2.3. Here readers are provided with learning objectives and are invited to carry out an evaluation of each one, assessing the degree to which they may be deemed educational.

Box 2.3 Skills and knowledge: acquisition or education?

1   To teach the children about the Four Pillars of Islam
2   To help children memorise the Ten Commandments
3   To test which pupils have learnt The Lord's Prayer
4   To encourage discussion about Francis of Assisi's decision to give away his riches to the poor
5   To explain the significance of the *menorah* to Jewish people

---

Discussion of learning objectives 1–5 (Box 2.3)

The kind of thinking inherent in learning objectives (2) and (3) is similar: to ensure pupils have acquired information which could lead to some future conditioning of attitudes. Of course, much depends on the purpose behind these objectives. It is quite possible that the intention is for the pupils to utilise the information in order to further personal reflection and understanding.

However, for many rote learning is neither natural nor motivating. The author remembers clearly from her own school days as a six year old having, along with the rest of the class, to learn the words of the patriotic song 'Rose of England' for a public performance on Empire Day. She was unable to recite it to the class, and the teacher sent her to the porches with the order that she should wash her face in order to wake up! What happened in the porches was not, however, what the teacher had intended, for there the little girl met some friends from other classes, and they spent some time chasing each other around the pegs! She remembers returning quietly and seriously to the classroom in mock repentance, but secretly triumphing. She learnt to detest that particular patriotic song, the words of which she never memorised, and the incident always springs to her mind whenever the former British Empire is mentioned. That was how the hidden curriculum influenced the content of her learning.

There is a serious danger lurking behind objectives (1) and (5), namely one of promoting *indifference*. Put simply, this is a method frequently found in our school system (and thus significant for wider society itself) of presenting material to pupils in such a way that they become distanced from it. In other words, it is presented impersonally, with the result that the children may well be led to think 'Oh, that is how those people behave, is it? All very interesting, but I cannot see what it has to do with me.' Attitudes of indifference are easily encouraged, even though this is not necessarily the intention of the teacher. Indeed, objectives (1) and (5), in their goal of expanding the pupils' horizons the better to understand other religions, seem on the surface to be remarkably well intentioned. The hope of the teacher could be that the children will gradually absorb the material presented, and that the beliefs and values inherent in it will inform their own developing value-system.

This is probably the type of thinking which underlay the whole practice of rote-learning, particularly during past decades. However, as the 'Rose of England' episode presented above illustrates, the opposite effect is even more likely to enjoy success. Children (as well as people) are remarkably resistant to any attempt to force on them information and attitudes which seem to be irrelevant.

Learning in whichever form it may be presented, is non-educational if it leads to a mere mechanical process of regurgitation. As students have often remarked to me, 'Yes, even a budgie can be taught to recite tables and, no doubt, the Lord's Prayer'. The question which needs asking is the extent to which the budgie that has successfully acquired this skill (if skill it happens to be) can be deemed to be *educated*? It is extremely doubtful whether it will be able to make use of its tables in calculating, for example, the cost of its seed.

Perhaps what is needed is a teaching method that presents material to pupils in ways that are likely to engage their curiosity and interest and which leads to genuine absorption of the material itself. This should result in the pupils questioning it and relating it to their own interests and experiences in order both to broaden and deepen their understanding. The material mentioned in objectives (1) and (5) could be used educationally – that is, in order to help pupils evaluate their own ideas and experiences in the light of the material presented to them. Some very rich, stimulating work could then be developed on the Five Pillars of Islam and on the symbolism of the *menorah*.

Closely linked to this is the *appropriateness* of lesson content. Piaget, writing copiously throughout the first half of this century, argued that children's chronological age was the all-important factor in determining what type of material they could deal with effectively, and his ideas were applied to the field of Religious Education by Ronald Goldman (1964; 1965). However, both Piagetian psychology and, therefore, the work of Goldman has been widely discredited (see, for example, Minney, 1985; Petrovich, 1988; Vidal, 1994; Ashton, 1997b, 1997c). Because of inherent weaknesses in Goldman's research into children's potential for 'religious thinking' (such as preconceived notions of what religion comprises and particularly about 'poetic' language), his theories have been largely superseded (see, for example, Ainsworth, 1983). What seems to be required is a much deeper perception of the factors that motivate for children (see Chapter 6 for full discussion and suggestions).

Learning objective (4) ('The acquisition of skills and knowledge') has the potential to be very effective educationally. What is significant here is the way in which the teacher apparently intends not only to provide the pupils with some information (that is, about Francis of Assisi's decision to cast away his wealth) but also to encourage them to engage in some critical discussion about it. Therefore, one would expect the children to use their knowledge about St Francis as a springboard to examine their own ideas about money, what it can buy, its real status and the things which they really treasure (see Boxes 10.1 and 10.2 for a development of this theme).

Let us return now to our discussion of the aims of education (see Box 2.1). Learning objective (7) ('the capacity to earn one's living') is, of course, largely utilitarian, although often stressed by politicians and the media as being a central concern of education. How far education is a prerequisite – that is a foundation of personality development – before vocational training should be undertaken is an extremely important point which could fruitfully be debated elsewhere.

The approach to education that I wish to encourage can perhaps best be illustrated through a metaphor (see also Chapter 4 for further discussion on the centrality of language in religious understanding). If education is understood in terms of a journey, we then need to reflect on various aspects of journeys. Some of these are given in Box 2.4, and readers are invited to consider these, and perhaps to add to them in order to determine how far the metaphor illuminates their perceptions of education.

Box 2.4 Word-field: education conceived in terms of a journey

motorways   petrol stations   maps   breakdowns   accidents
passengers   luggage   road repairs   snarl-ups   junctions
vehicles   road-signs   overtaking lanes   driving test   preparation
excitement   route   challenge   danger

Readers will be left with this exercise for a while in the anticipation that they might find it a useful springboard in their reading of the remainder of this chapter. Full discussion will be reserved for Chapter 4, where additional metaphors will be discussed. For now, I wish to focus on one aspect of journeys which is not included in Box 2.4, and which is significant for education: the subject of *destinations*. Where could education be sensibly and realistically envisaged as moving towards?

Education and the five-fold attitudes of respect

Let me here introduce readers to certain distinctive characteristics of education, and hopefully of the educated person. These characteristics are summed up as learning objectives (6) of Box 2.1 (viz. 'Learning to respect beauty, truth, others, the environment and oneself'). The suggestion is that it could be useful to peruse the list of people given in Box 2.5, asking which ones could reasonably be described as being 'educated'.

Box 2.5 Word-field: who might be the educated ones?

farrier   child in the Reception class   primitive herdsman   primary school teacher   shopkeeper   university professor   caretaker assembly-line worker   agricultural labourer   housewife and mother   radiographer   violinist   professional gardener   bank manager   medical doctor   minister of religion   nurse

---

Discussion of Box 2.5

On the basis of the information provided above, and without having met any of the people listed solely by occupation, I would not consider myself to be in a position to decide whether any of them were educated. Indeed, I would not feel able to make any assertion other than that some of them had possibly enjoyed greater opportunities than others for *becoming* educated. Unless one is in a position to observe for oneself, and thereby ascertain another person's attitude towards life in all its entirety, it is impossible to know who can, in all fairness, be characterised in this way.

Many people might consider the university professor would stand a good chance of being an 'educated' person, but that of course depends upon one's experience of university professors. Certainly, the primitive herdsman could well be extremely wise, whilst the Reception class child, on account of his/her short time on this earth, will probably have had very limited opportunities to have had any enthusiasms and curiosities stifled by life's experiences. The all-important question concerns how one learns to distinguish the educated from the uneducated, or to put the dilemma another way: *what criteria can we identify which might assist us in the task?*

It is possible to do this, and furthermore I would suggest that from their Reception in the school system, development of the following five-fold aspects of respect within each child should be the aim of the teacher. Full discussion is developed on this theme elsewhere (Watson, 1987, 14–16), but I shall expand on it here since the following chapters of the book aim to show how these five aspects of respect can be central in guiding the teacher through his/her teaching, and Religious Education specifically.

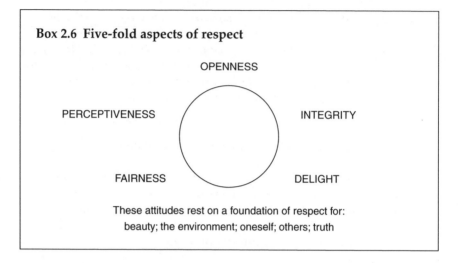

Box 2.6 Five-fold aspects of respect

OPENNESS

PERCEPTIVENESS   INTEGRITY

FAIRNESS   DELIGHT

These attitudes rest on a foundation of respect for:
beauty; the environment; oneself; others; truth

If the central circle stands for the person, and the surrounding attributes signify the five-fold nature of respect, that is, attitudes that are characteristic of the educated person, then each attribute can be used as a criterion when making an assessment of a pupil's progress educationally. I shall now discuss each of these attributes in some depth.

(a) Openness   This refers to an attitude of mind which is not closed by such phenomena as complacency, smugness, conceit, prejudice or feeling that one definitely can be absolutely certain about anything at all, except trivial details of everyday living. In other words, this attitude is open to new insights and ideas and is receptive to the possibility of, for example, new evidence leading to departures from 'established' doctrines and beliefs held for centuries. An example could be openness to the possibility that the standard chronology for Ancient Egypt might need considerable readjustment in order to accommodate fresh insights and discoveries. Even work with very young children needs to have built into it this open approach, in order that pupils have every opportunity of learning its importance from the time that they begin their career in school.

(b) Integrity   This attitude of mind reflects a concern for all that is realistic, honest, sympathetic and generous. It implies a willingness to accept each individual in a spirit of openness, recognising individuality that goes beyond mere role-playing.

(c) Delight   The capacity to show delight when experiencing aspects of living is central to the educated person. This is because delight is in itself motivating, whether in the search for knowledge and the excitement felt when arriving at fresh insights, or in feeling the motivation for satisfying one's curiosity by further investigations. A component of delight is often the capacity to perceive the ridiculous and to share with others the pleasure this can bring. All of these attributes work in levels of human psychology, from the Early Years schoolchild to the university professor.

(d) Fairness   All young children – as well as the not so young – will show indignation at anything they conceive to be unfair. It is as if human beings have an innate sense of fairness. On many occasions the young child will be heard to declare 'It's not fair!' The assumption seems to be that things *ought to be fair*. Irrespective of whether or not this is true, it certainly is the case that justice (which is what fairness really implies) is something that has to be continually striven for. As the history of the human race shows, injustice will quickly take over, with devastating effects, when opportunities permit. In religious terms, this is the fight between Good and Evil, wrong and right, and is central to any programme of education.

(e) Perceptiveness   This refers to the capacity both to formulate one's own insights and to acknowledge those of other people. It includes imaginative and creative reflective thought (as opposed to conjuring up mere fantasy or unrealistic notions) which could lead to new and exciting developments, as well as appreciation of the good in people and of that which is beautiful. Attributes such as these help one see beyond disguises, whether presented in human or inanimate terms. In other words, the perceptive person is not easily fooled!

If these five-fold aspects of respect are applied to the foundation of human experience – that is, beauty, environment, oneself, others and truth in its widest dimensions – the result is likely to be a wise, enquiring mind, deriving its richness through a search for justice and tempered with realism because of the gift of humour. This is the real purpose behind the brand of education advanced in this book.

Education through Religion

How does the five-fold model of respect interrelate with Religious Education? In order that education through the lens of religion can take place at levels beyond the simplistic or superficial, the model needs to be placed at the heart of teaching. In this way it will provide the life-blood of learning programmes with curiosity and the excitement gradually to understand more about the mystery at the heart of religion, thus stimulating motivation. This can be perceived as follows.

1   *Religious Education and truth* Educationally effective Religious Education encourages, and perhaps initiates, young children (and the not so young) into a search for truth by helping them to become aware of and reflect on the truth claims that lie at the heart of religion (see Box 2.7). It is these claims which provide the yardstick referred to earlier (pp. 1, 7) against which personal experience can be evaluated.

2   *Religious Education and other people* This necessitates an awareness of the implications for human behaviour of the truth claims of religion. This is a two-way process, because how one's own behaviour affects others holds further implications not only for wider society, but also the local community. For example, in School 1 David was shouted at by his teacher for not joining in the singing of a hymn during school worship. She defended her behaviour later by saying she thought of hymn-singing as a means of discipline. In School 2, however, children were invited to join in the singing if they wished to do so, otherwise to listen to the words others sang and to think hard about their meaning. What would be the likely effects of these two approaches on David and his fellow-pupils, in contrast to those in the other school? What guidance do the truth claims of religions offer? Undoubtedly, in the case of David, to foster a spirit of rebellion which is completely opposed to the search for beauty (see also point (5) below).

3   *Religious Education and oneself* The case study of Mandy illustrates this point (see p. 24). The quality of one's life is of vital importance not only for the people who are influenced one way or another by it, but also for the development of one's own personality.

4   *Religious Education and the environment* The truth claims at the heart of religion point towards both individual and corporate responsibility for careful use and nurture of the planet on which we both live and depend for life itself. People are therefore endowed with the task of working together as stewards for the well-being of creation.

5   *Religious Education and beauty* A growing appreciation of what is beautiful and attempts to foster it in its many dimensions reside at the heart of Religious Education. These dimensions include a love and fascination with colour, an awareness of harmony and rhythm, a love of order, aesthetically satisfying design, and an adherence to honesty, sincerity and personal integrity. Rejected are such phenomena as violence, hatred, jealousy and greed.

Box 2.7 Truth claims of religion

1 That a spirit of creative energy (God, Allah, for example) which is concerned with Creation, pervades the universe and is responsible for the way in which the world functions. In other words, that God is responsible for the working of scientific laws.

2 That God maintains the whole of Creation, rather than merely being its creator.

3 That prayer is about communication with God – being in God's presence. Thus prayerful activity involves a heightened sensitivity and awareness that one is close to God.

4 That prayer is about being aware of closeness to God, rather than using God as an instrument that will, perhaps, grant favours.

5 Because of our limited perceptions and the impossibility of knowing everything that there is to know, our capacity to understand God is severely limited. This is why metaphorical language and signs and symbols are used by religions to indicate the reality of God.

6 That the present, material world – that is, the world that is subject to physical laws, is profoundly influenced by the spiritual dimension. Therefore, to see a division between the two is grossly to distort and diminish a reality of which people throughout the ages have been acutely aware, irrespective of culture, geography or historical time.

7 That God is able to override scientific laws at any time when it is appropriate to do so. Therefore, miracles consist of experiences when this 'overriding' seems to have taken place.

8 Prayer can be answered in both negative and positive ways. To reject the reality of the power of prayer on the grounds that prayers were apparently unanswered is to miss the point. Prayer is answered, but not necessarily in the way requested.

9 The reality of suffering, in all its dimensions, is a mystery.

10 Life in the material dimension of reality, although integrated with the spiritual, is a means of preparing for the possibility of a better future in a realm that transcends suffering, sorrow, pain and other negativities. In effect, it is a 'training ground' that provides opportunities for immense spiritual growth and awareness.

Let us turn now to the second part of the discussion, which concerns what experiences of religion could offer this educational journey.

Religion in education

There follows a discussion of specific ways of conceiving of Religious Education which have developed over the past few decades and which continue to exert influence over the ways in which the subject is treated in primary schools. Please refer now to Box 2.8. Readers might find it helpful to consider what influences could have led to the formulation of any of the following notions of Religious Education.

Box 2.8 Approaches to primary school Religious Education

The 'confessional' approach   This is the traditional way of teaching Christianity, although applicable to all other religions. This approach is characterised by initiation into a particular form of religion, usually without debate.

Explicit Religious Education   Lessons in RE which introduce pupils to obviously religious material, e.g. narrative, prayer or study of scripture.

Implicit Religious Education   A term which is often associated with ideas originating from the theories of Goldman, Implicit RE includes 'life themes' e.g. 'People Who Help Us', or other topics which, whilst not explicitly religious, are thought to introduce pupils to religious attitudes and ethics.

The phenomenological approach   In everyday language, this approach is often called 'multi-faith' RE. At a theoretical level, it originated from the work of Ninian Smart and other early members of the Shap Working Party. Basically, the approach aims to give understanding of seven dimensions of religion: the mythological, doctrinal, ethical, ritual, experiential, social and artistic/material. Thus it is hoped to help pupils gain respect for the religious dimension of human life.

The experiential approach   In some respects this can be understood as a development of implicit RE. Largely based on the work of David Hay, the approach attempts to provide opportunities for pupils to experience – in non-explicitly religious terms – dilemmas or other human concerns that are believed to underlie religious experience – for example, human anxiety, self-consciousness and the inner life which one so frequently attempts to conceal.

The evaluative approach   An approach which is based on the five-fold search for respect (see p. 16). It takes seriously religious truth claims,

---

the development of religious concepts and the search for commitment, and it encourages a capacity to cope with controversial issues. It respects awareness of the mystery at the heart of reality.

It is possible to assess the educational significance of these approaches to Religious Education by asking a single question of all of them and applying criteria for assessment. There are many questions which could be asked. Of great significance to the teaching of religion is how to cope creatively with controversy, and children are entitled from the earliest age to appreciate that religion is a controversial area of human experience. Therefore, the question to be asked by the above approaches of teaching Religious Education is: *Which form of Religious Education can best promote a creative approach to controversy?*

The criteria (or queries) against which the question will be assessed are as follows:

- *Comprehensiveness*: Is it open to new ideas and insights?
- *Explicability*: Does it explain anything, or offer new insights?
- *Beneficial consequences*: Is it likely to be helpful to life generally?
- *Workability*: Is it likely to work, in practice?

Readers might find it helpful to apply the criteria themselves, and then compare the results with those given in Box 2.9.

Box 2.9 Which form of RE can best promote a creative approach to controversy?

Approach	Comprehen-siveness	Explicability	Beneficial consequences	Workability
Confessional ('We're right')	No; dogmatic and not concerned with pupils' own insights.	No; selective and authority-based.	Yes; can give some in-depth understanding. No; negative to others' views.	No; sets up rival groups.
Phenomeno-logical ('No-one is right; we are just different')	No; fails to take truth claims seriously.	No; empirically based: sees religions as external practices.	Yes; can convey information to help tolerance develop. No; superficial.	No; excludes those who might be dogmatic.

Approach	Comprehensiveness	Explicability	Beneficial consequences	Workability
Experiential ('We're all right – but only for ourselves')	No; fails to relate to public discourse about religion.	No; vague about what religion is.	Yes; gives opportunities to relate to, and express parts of personality often closed. No; can lead to introspection.	No; insists on purely private nature of religious experience.
Evaluative ('We have to work towards being right, trusting in what we think we know')	Yes; presumes all have insights and tries to develop them.	Yes; it takes religion seriously.	Yes; accepts the fact of controversy.	Yes; it debars none and affirms all.

Discussion on approaches to Religious Education (Box 2.9)

Every society initiates the young into its beliefs and values system, whether religious or secular. Of course, the purpose of education is to ensure that the search for knowledge provides opportunities for students of all ages to investigate and assess for themselves the bodies of wisdom and beliefs which underlie civilisations. Notions that education can be neutral are necessarily mistaken (see Hulmes, 1979; Ashton and Watson, 1998).

As late as 1967, the belief was expressed that the young should be initiated into Christianity: 'They [the children] should be taught to know and love God and to practise in the school community the virtues appropriate to their age and environment' (Plowden, 1967, 207). Further, it was stressed that: 'Children should not be unnecessarily involved in religious controversy. They should not be confused by being taught to doubt before faith is established' (ibid., 207). These statements typify the 'confessional' approach to Religious Education. However, there has been a move away from this position, which is often claimed to have developed because of the increasingly multi-cultural nature of British society during the second half of the twentieth century especially. Although a broadly Christian-based culture remains dominant, largely because of the long history of Christianity in Western Europe, communities of followers of other faiths, particularly Hindu, Islamic, Jewish, Sikh and Buddhist, form a significant part of the population in many areas of the country.

It is not, perhaps, surprising that teachings concerning faiths in addition to Christianity have become firmly entrenched in the school curriculum. Indeed, the Model Syllabuses of Religious Education, produced as guidelines for Local Education Authorities in their efforts to produce their own Agreed Syllabus of Religious Education, state clearly that children in schools must be introduced to a variety of the great world religions during their education (see Appendix A).

However, the question which has to be asked concerns how this can best be done, and with what purpose. Implicit Religious Education is now widely recognised as being vague, often without any religious content whatsoever, and overwhelmed by erroneous assumptions concerning the incapacity of young children for religious thinking (Goldman, 1964, 1965, and comments on these researches by Ashton 1997b, 1997c), whilst explicit Religious Education, as presented under the confessional approach, often comprised no more than attempts to 'place before [its] pupils a rational statement of Christian belief, suited of course to their age and abilities' (Curtis, 1953, 382).

However, readers might well detect an assumption underlying this statement. The clue is given in the use of the word 'rational': could the fact/belief dichotomy described earlier be influencing thinking here? It is hardly surprising that the phenomenological approach to Religious Education (see above, Box 2.8) as it has developed in schools, has become characterised by attempts to teach 'the facts' about religions. As pointed out by Watson (1993, 44–46), there has been considerable criticism of this particular approach to Religious Education, widespread though the method is in primary schools. Many of these criticisms are extremely serious, especially the one that argues phenomenology has stripped Religious Education of any examination of the truth claims which lie at the heart of religious experience and which ought to form the central core of teaching.

Of equal significance, although more subtle, is the influence of secularism in this approach to Religious Education. By distancing pupils from discussion of faith on account of an over-emphasis on, for example, religious rituals and artefacts which can be understood to comprise efforts to be neutral in teaching (or even to make religion respectably 'factual'), it is all too easy to create the impression that religion is what *other* people engage in, rather than something that could have personal relevance. In this way, as pointed out by Hulmes (1979), efforts at neutrality very quickly become, in effect, an initiation into secularism, or agnosticism.

The Experiential approach aimed to focus on personal experience, thus preparing foundations for the introduction of explicitly religious material in order that its relevance would be apparent to students (Hay *et al.*, 1990). However, many of the activities offered under this approach require extremely sensitive handling by teachers, such is their personal impact. Moreover, because of their 'implicit' nature, they often seem to fit more appropriately within programmes of personal and social education than within Religious Education.

Bearing in mind the evaluative approach to Religious Education, based as it is on the five-fold aspects of respect (Box 2.6), the following is offered in the belief that study of these, and associated topics, focus on an investigation of religious truth claims in ways that avoid the pitfalls of other approaches to the teaching of religion. All of these cases are developed later in the book.

1   *The development of personal integrity – the case of Mandy*   Mandy, a five-year-old child in the Reception class, upset a child by tearing his painting at the end of a lesson, and kicking over a pot of water on to the classroom floor. When the student taking the class scolded her, the child retorted, 'My mum says God always forgives you when you are naughty. It doesn't matter how often I get into trouble.' How should the student or teacher respond?

2   *Religion as a balance against materialism – the case of the Buddha*   Prince Siddhartha, as a boy and young man, was never allowed to see anything of life which could have upset him. Even dead flowers were removed from the palace gardens so he would not experience death. However, as a young man he became bored with his life of luxury in the palace and its grounds, and ordered a servant to take him outside of the walls of his 'prison'. The first thing he saw was a beggar, and this experience led him on a new road of discovery (see also Box 10.4).

3   *Religion as an antidote to stereotyping – the Hindu theory of reincarnation*   A student told me that a six-year-old pupil had picked up a stereotyped version of the theory of reincarnation. He said, 'Miss, is it true that if your granny dies and comes back as a beetle, and you stamp on the beetle, you have killed your granny again?' How should the teacher respond? (see p. 6)

4   *Religious insights into personal relationships*   As a boy, Joseph was attacked by his older brothers and sold into slavery. His father grieved bitterly, believing him to be dead. Years later, when the brothers went to Egypt to buy corn during a famine in their country, they found themselves bowing before the brother they had mistreated years before! How should Joseph respond – by forgiving or taking revenge? (See Box A3.)

5   *Religion as a spiritual journey*   Henry of Coquet, a Danish Prince, felt he had received a calling to leave his life as a soldier and to live alone, as a hermit, in order to be able to devote all of his time to God. He set up home on a lonely island off the coast of Northumberland and began an extraordinary spiritual journey which led him to be buried alongside famous kings (see Box A7).

Conclusion

Studies of religion which can be described as being truly educational aim at introducing pupils to the insights and wisdoms of the human race which have been conceptualised within a religious context. The nature of these is obviously subjective, but the foregoing discussion has tried to show that subjectivity in itself is not something necessarily unhelpful or inferior to data which are assumed to be objective. Rather, different criteria are needed in any assessments made, and may be drawn from the wealth of personal experience each individual undergoes throughout life.

The insights and wisdoms referred to above offer standards against which to understand one's dilemmas and problems. As mentioned earlier, serious reflection will contribute to an all-round assessment both of one's own situation, and the extent to which the insights and wisdoms called upon offer sound guidance.

We have considered the nature of Religious Education, then the main misconceptions which tend to impede effective teaching of the subject, and most importantly of all an approach to the subject which should free the mind of the teacher who wishes to present religious ideas to pupils openly and with the intention of helping them think freely about them. I turn in the next section to two vitally important subjects which need to be the central focus of teaching if children are to be helped to move forward in their reflections on religious insight and wisdom: these are *language use* and *conceptual development in religion*.

Part II

RELIGION IN EDUCATION

The previous section discussed common misconceptions surrounding Religious Education, and their influence on the subject's development in the curriculum of schools. Central to the problem are popular movements in thinking and especially the way in which pseudo-scientific ideas contributed to a false 'fact' vs. 'belief' division. Having argued what the subject was *not* concerned with, discussion moved on to investigate how Religious Education can be planned in order to help children become aware of the large bodies of wisdom which constitute religious insights, and the educational value of these in providing a yardstick against which personal experiences and ideas may be measured.

Part II begins by investigating a major theme closely related to Religious Education, that is, the role of language in the development of religious thought and understanding. The approach to Religious Education advocated in this book is the presentation and discussion of a broad range of religious insights and the large compendium of human wisdom that has resulted, rather than merely an examination of religious artefacts, buildings and rituals. In order to support this approach it is vital that pupils are helped to interpret symbolic language which is so necessary for the communication of deep insight.

The importance of metaphor in language for conceptual development in religion is discussed in Chapter 3. Here the focus in on a theme central to education in religion, whichever religious tradition is being studied: that is, concepts of God. Chapter 4 develops the theme by exploring some concepts that are basic to the understanding of religion, most importantly the meaning of 'God' and how people attempt to express their ideas. This is done by providing examples of lesson content and associated discussion material.

Chapter 5 discusses possible approaches to conversing with children, especially when difficult 'ultimate questions' are asked, enquiring what the role of the teacher ought to be – should we attempt to provide answers to such questions, or is there a more educational approach?

The section concludes by looking at factors that have been found motivating for pupils as they are introduced to religious narrative, insights and ideas. This involves examining signs and symbols and the importance of the sense of mystery which is always central to learning.

3

LANGUAGE DEVELOPMENT AND RELIGIOUS EDUCATION

Introduction

The development of children's language is central to their growing understanding of religion. This is because, language being the most commonly used medium through which people both think and communicate, it is essential that the ways in which it is used in the expression of religious insights and ideas are taught and understood, and there is no better place to begin than in the Early Years classroom.

This chapter, therefore, looks specifically at metaphor in language: what it is and why it is particularly important for communicating and understanding religion. Suggestions are then made for approaches in the teaching of young children.

What is metaphor?

Metaphor is one of the quickest and most effective aids to thinking and communication that exist. This is because it has a visual aspect and does not depend upon hosts of words in order to make important points. Above all, because of its creative nature, the person who undertakes the interpretation of metaphors becomes involved in the intriguing task of reflecting further by drawing upon personal experience. There is mystery surrounding metaphors which is motivating in itself (see Chapter 6), and the possibility of uncovering many meanings and dealing with them can become an exciting adventure.

Let us, for example, study the first line from Alfred Noyes' poem 'The Highwayman'. The poet sets the scene with this line: 'The moon was a ghostly galleon tossed upon cloudy seas'. The poet tells us much about the background scene to 'The Highwayman', and he uses a powerful metaphor in order to do so. The line seems to be about the moon and galleons, clouds and the sea. How does one recognise that Noyes is not using straight description? By drawing upon our experience of moons and of galleons, we known that a moon cannot really *be* a galleon! After all, a galleon is a ship and a moon is one of earth's satellites. Another clue to the use of metaphors is contained in the words 'cloudy seas'. How can seas be cloudy? The reader is therefore enticed by the mystery at the heart of the metaphors to search for aspects of moons and galleons, clouds and seas, which are similar. The two aspects of the metaphors interact and inform each other, with the result the reader is provided with the possibility of attaining heightened sensitivity and insights concerning the appearance of the moon and clouds on the particular night in question. The result is for the poet successfully to 'set the scene', or communicate the atmosphere against which the events of the narrative are to unfold.

Metaphor is, therefore, very helpful in stimulating abstract thinking. By using metaphor, even very small children can cope with complex notions and begin to give expression to multi-faceted insights which defy the literal use of language. Here is an example, drawn from the Sikh religion, of a metaphor used to describe the power of God: 'Thou turnest men like me from blades of grass into mountains' (Ferguson, 1997, 144). This is a vivid means of communicating, perhaps, the insight that God can transform the weak into the brave, the feeble into the powerful, but readers might like to consider other possibilities, too!

There is a very important misunderstanding, however, which needs to be guarded against. This is that if we talk literally we are speaking of *facts*, whilst if we use metaphor it is just *imagination* – that what is being described so vividly is 'just a metaphor', something that does not really exist. For example, James Lovelock, when defending his theory of Planet Gaia, asserted that he was well aware that when he was describing the ecosystem as being 'alive' because it behaved like a living organism, he was speaking metaphorically, but continued by emphasising that the theory was 'real science' and no 'mere metaphor' (Lovelock, 1991, 6). There are several points to raise here. It would seem that Lovelock has fallen into the trap of considering that metaphors indicate something lacking existence, or reality. Second, he implies by the use of the phrase 'mere metaphor' that metaphors are somehow inferior to what they are signifying, in this instance his theory concerning the ecosystem. Of course, metaphors are devices for both thinking and communicating in language, and ought not to be confused with the insight itself.

A further misunderstanding is to believe metaphor to be simply a figure of speech, something that can be taught and learnt as a tiny part of English – a small aspect of how language is used in poetry or prose. Metaphor is far more than this. Research by Lakoff and Johnson (1980) has pointed out that metaphors, ranging from the simple to the complex, are the 'building bricks' of language itself. We constantly use bits of what is familiar in order to shed new light on what is new, or even to communicate fresh insights on the old.

It might be helpful, at this point, to refer to the metaphor 'Education is a Journey' (see p. 14), and apply the various aspects of journeys provided in

Box 2.4 to 'education'. How far do they help illuminate one's perceptions of the function of education? Does it make sense to argue that as 'Education is a journey' is 'just a metaphor', that education does not therefore exist? Does thinking of education through an alternative metaphor – 'Education is a business' – alter your understanding of its role? Which metaphor do you think the more appropriate?

The reason why metaphor is so important is that our experiences of life and of the world, of relationships and of being an individual, are much greater than we can put into words. Life and experience are like the air through which we fly, whilst words are like one footstep after another – incredibly slow and more limited. Just think of the soaring ability of the swallow and compare it with a person walking. What happens when the persons comes to a cliff edge? By contrast, what does the swallow do?

This capacity of metaphor to soar far beyond words is particularly important in religious thinking because the concept of God is infinitely beyond the limitations of human language – we can never convey through words exactly what 'God' implies. However, there is a danger lurking here. Because of their fluidity, metaphors can be interpreted inappropriately, as well as in ways that are helpful. This can lead to serious misunderstandings as they can play a large part in misinforming people about what religious insights are trying to convey.

Here is a metaphor of God that is regularly used within Christian cultures and which exerts a profound influence on the religious understanding of everyone living in the Western world, whether adherents of Christianity, of another great world religion, or of none at all:

- *God is our father.*

Please spend a few minutes developing your thoughts on this, that is, examining what the metaphor implies about God, in the light of your understanding of fathers, before reading on.

Discussion

There are two categories into which your comments could well be classified. These are:

1 *Bodily/spatial aspects of fathers*, and therefore of God: that is, that God has a body, perhaps of an old man, and can be located in space somewhere (perhaps among the clouds) in a 'place' which is called heaven, mainly in Christian scripture, although not exclusively.
2 *Relationship aspect of fathers*, and therefore of God: that is, how good fathers relate to their family and the community generally, by providing stability, shelter, loving care, defence, wisdom and comfort.

Please look at any notes you made in response to the metaphor 'God is our father', and spend a few moments classifying them under (1) or (2).

The notions described in (1) typify popular notions of Christian culture, and are prevalent throughout the Western world. Although emanating from misunderstood aspects of Christian doctrine, they are not Christian in content, and unfortunately are possessed of the power of undermining religious faith, irrespective of the particular religion in question. Thinking of God as a man – that is, focusing on bodily aspects of fathers and locating them spatially, is known as *crude anthropomorphism*. This way of thinking is reinforced, unfortunately, by the whole gamut of religious culture in the Western world – pictures of God as an old man in the sky, the opening words of the Lord's Prayer, 'Our father which art in heaven', and the words of countless hymns and prayers. Yet this way of perceiving the fatherhood of God is not scriptural – it is a misinterpretation. The *relationship* aspects of fathers is what the metaphor is pointing towards, not spatial or bodily ones.

It is, of course, quite understandable that people should grasp at the more tangible aspects of the metaphor, particularly as they tend to be reinforced throughout Christian art and literature, and yet they are unhelpful for developing adequate concepts of the deity, whichever religion is under investigation. Unfortunately, crude anthropomorphism runs the risk of encouraging people to dismiss the idea of God as pure fantasy – as indicated, perhaps, by Yuri Gagarin who stated on his return from a voyage into space, 'I didn't see God'.

There is, however, another danger in thinking of God in terms of crude anthropomorphism. It is closely connected with one's concept of metaphor, and this danger is a double-edged sword! These dangers are:

1 The whole idea of God is rejected because the 'old man in the sky' mental image seems to be ludicrous, especially in the light of modern scientific understanding.
2 A defensive attitude asserts itself, which defends dogmatically the literal interpretation of the metaphor.

As we have seen, however, both positions stem from the same misunderstanding, and lead to a similar obstruction to the advancement of thought. A central role in the religious education of young children is to help them diversify their thinking of God, whichever world religion is under study, by examining a variety of metaphors which provide checks and balances to our understanding. Some specific, practical ideas are suggested in the following chapter (pp. 49–60) on how this could be attempted.

Returning now to the general discussion on metaphor – it is precisely here that the misunderstanding of seeing metaphor as mere 'imagination', or 'made up', compared with 'fact that is true' needs to be avoided.

Perhaps the easiest way of seeing this is to think of metaphor as a signpost which directs our thoughts towards or away from truth. A signpost to SWINDON which actually points to the road leading away from SWINDON to OXFORD would be leading the traveller astray. Equally confusing would be a signpost pointing to OXFORD which led to a network of small roads which did not have signposts – they are needed in order to help the bewildered traveller approach the journey's end. The same applies to metaphor. If the metaphor leads people to images of something that is illuminating and truthful, then it is apt and helpful – a true metaphor. If, however, the images it conjures up are misleading and mistaken, confusing and untruthful, then the metaphor is a false one which needs to be either corrected, adjusted or, in the last instance, replaced.

Box 3.1 below provides sets of metaphors which could be used with young children. They could be asked to discuss them with their friends and decide which ideas are the best for describing the person or thing in question.

Box 3.1 Sorting out ideas: true, false or somewhere in between?

Snow White was:
- a rose
- treasure
- a rainbow

Footballers are:
- stars
- supermen
- tin gods

Computers are:
- brain-boxes
- teachers
- a file

Money is:
- treasure
- a worry
- dangerous

God is:
- a man in the sky
- a powerful force
- a magnet
- treasure

School is:
- a prison
- a sunny day
- an exciting trip
- a battlefield

The ideas given above, and others created by the teacher, could be typed and mounted as work-cards for children to discuss in groups. It is stressed that the objective of any such work would be to generate ideas and genuine discussion in depth, not to arrive at definite answers. (See Chapter 5 for further discussion.)

Metaphors can be used to powerful, and even terrifying, effect. For example, Adolf Hitler, voicing his twisted ideology of Nazism, described the Jewish people as 'a sick appendix to be removed'. The utter distortion of this vivid image shows graphically the power of metaphor and the need to help people become aware of its ability to influence perceptions and opinions, and to sort out the appropriate from the inappropriate, the ludicrous from the sane.

To use another example, taken from Box 3.1 above: if we assert that 'School is a battlefield' what are the contradictory notions that could be conveyed? One person could associate 'battlefield' with horror and carnage; whilst for another it could imply honour and glory.

In the following section I shall turn to the interesting subject of layers of meaning in metaphors and conclude by providing examples of how work on them could be planned for young children.

Levels of meaning in language

A mistake made by Goldman (1964, 1965) was his contention that it is wrong to accept metaphors at their literal level (that is, the obvious, surface level). This led him to conclude that, as children of primary school age were, apparently, unable to deal with metaphors other than at literal levels of meaning, they ought not to be introduced to the majority of Biblical narratives which comprised most Religious Education lessons at that time.

However, Goldman's claims were mistaken in two respects. The first, his assumption concerning metaphor, is discussed below, whilst the second is included in the last section of this chapter which suggests practical activities for young children to introduce them to the study of metaphor.

Metaphor can be envisaged in terms of the depth of the ocean: it is possible to swim on the surface or to dive to ever increasing depths in order to penetrate the mysteries of the ocean. All activities – whether carried out in shallow waters or in the deep are legitimate, of course. However, the deeper a diver is able to go, the more exciting and stimulating the activity is likely to be.

Interpreting metaphors is similar. There is no reason to suppose *all* literal interpretations of metaphors to be false. The following is a case in point. Please consider the following, taken from a six year old child's writing:

- *'My heart was singing as I danced across the lawn'* (Susan).

What did the child mean? When I asked her if anyone could hear her heart as it sang, she laughed, and said she meant she felt very happy, just like songs are happy. Susan had actually plunged below the literal level of the meaning of her metaphor because she knew her heart had *not* been engaging in physical singing. Nevertheless, as her friend said to her, maybe her heart had been singing but she could not hear it because it was inside her. I then suggested to the little girls that the happiness they felt could best be described as singing, and they both agreed.

If we examine the Biblical accounts of Jesus' temptation in the wilderness, we are told that during his stay in the latter he was followed around by Satan, or the devil. Readers of this narrative are faced with deciding whether or not Satan took physical form and could have been seen walking with Jesus in the wilderness, or whether picture language (or metaphor) was being used as a depiction of the force that was apparently tempting Jesus to do wrong.

In his writings, Goldman (1964, 172–174) argued that children perceive the devil in three basic stages: first, as a 'bad man'; second, as 'something supernatural'; and third, as something real which is part of human nature – evil becomes personified in sinful action, for example. The significance of these 'stages' for this line of thinking is to assume that the lower the stage, the more faulty is the thinking underlying it. Therefore, to think of the devil as a 'man', or as something supernatural, is to think in ways that are inferior to stage three.

However, who is in a position to argue dogmatically that 'Satan' was merely 'bad thoughts' inside Jesus' head? Could the devil have been personified in this case? It is certainly possible to argue that Hitler became an embodiment of evil! The point I am trying to make is that thinking of evil as a person is not necessarily unhelpful – it can be a very early way in which the human mind begins to reflect and think about the problem presented. Much that is similar can, of course, be said about anthropomorphic concepts of God (see discussion on pp. 46–7). There is not necessarily anything wrong with anthropomorphism. Where the notion becomes misleading is when it becomes *crude* anthropomorphism – that is, God as an old man in the sky, or Satan as a horned creature carrying a pitchfork! Especially in popular perceptions of Christianity such images abound.

However, the task of the teacher consists not so much in ensuring pupils do not become acquainted with metaphorical literature too early (as argued by Goldman, for example), but rather in ensuring that throughout their education they are provided with opportunities to explore ideas, whether they are presented in prose, verse, panting, sculpture, figures or music.

Diving below the surface meaning: introducing young children to metaphor

As indicated above, theories from the past few decades have argued for the apparent inability of young children to think in the abstract or, more specifically, to be able to deal with metaphorical language. However, work by Lakoff and Johnson (1980) has shown that everyday language is pervaded by conventional metaphors which, because they are so familiar, are automatically interpreted at levels beyond the literal. It is here that teachers can find a starting point from which to guide young children towards poetic metaphors.

Starting points: conventional metaphors

Here are some examples of children's speech which include conventional metaphors: the latter have been indicated in italics.

- I *went across* to my gran's. [Meaning, not literally across a road, for example, but 'across' into a different atmosphere. This particular grandmother lived two houses away, on the same side of the road as the speaker.]
- Dad has just *put my pocket money up*. [Meaning more money is now being given: 'up' is used as indicating 'more', or even 'better' – e.g. a high pile of money is better than one which is low!]
- My dad has his *ups and downs*. [Meaning mood alterations: 'ups' being positive occasions, and 'downs' being negative, times to be wary of him.]
- *Cut it out*. [Meaning 'stop doing that' – eradicate it, as one would remove a diseased plant from a garden.]

Many more examples of conventional metaphors such as these can be found elsewhere (for example, Lakoff and Johnson, 1980; Deignan, 1995; Ashton, 1997a). At their most basic, conventional metaphors involve a subtle manipulation of words, playing on their possible meanings and merging those on borderlines. This practice is, of course, exemplified in children's love of riddles and jokes. In Box 3.2 are some well-known examples which, together with others that are similar, could usefully be discussed with children, particularly those in Year 2.

Box 3.2 Riddles as an introduction to metaphor

What has teeth but cannot bite?	Answer: a comb. Discuss with the children how a comb can 'bite' – e.g. move through hair, as teeth in the mouth can chew food.
What has an eye but cannot see?	Answer: a needle. The eye is a passageway of the body into the brain; the eye of a needle is a passageway through which thread is pushed.
What has legs but cannot move without help?	Answer: a chair, table, etc. Here legs are thought of as a type of stand: we stand on our feet which are attached to our legs, just as the seat of a chair 'stands' on its legs. Pictures of decorative legs of antique furniture could be shown to the children, e.g. 'ball and claw' styles.

The suggestion is that teachers could ask children to provide their own examples, and to discuss them with either their friends or the teacher in the above way. Alternatively, riddles could be printed on to sets of cards of one colour, and the solutions on cards of a different colour. Then the children's task would be to find the most appropriate solution.

In Box 3.3 are provided some religious metaphors. These were used by two students with a vertically grouped Early Years class, and some of the ideas of the children are included. The student teachers, Andrew and Sarah, worked with individuals and small groups, and reported that the work was well within the range of the children, who responded to the invitation to discuss with enthusiasm.

Box 3.3 Some examples of religious metaphors

Metaphor	*Possible interpretations*
Lord, our dagger, arrow, spear and sword (Sikh religion)	God provides us with a means of defence against evil, or wickedness. (Some five year olds suggested God might help you to win football matches.)
The Lord is My Shepherd (Judaism/ Christianity)	God will look after us as a shepherd cares for his flock of sheep. (A six year old suggested God was always looking after us and making sure we were safe from strangers.)
From end to end of the earth he stamps out war (Judaism)	God will put an end to war. (A seven year old suggested God does not like to see people fighting.)
From darkness lead me to light! (Hinduism)	Perhaps asking Brahman to take away suffering, pain, etc. (A six year old said 'Darkness gives you the creeps, but it goes away when you switch on your bedside lamp.')
Hail to you Ptah, Lord of Life! (Ancient Egypt)	The god Ptah has responsibility for the creation of life, rather than death. (A group of six year olds suggested the Ancient Egyptians enjoyed living and thanked their god for it.)

Metaphor	Possible interpretations
Allah, the all-knowing (Islam)	Allah (God) knows all that happens throughout the universe. (Some five year olds said God knows all about you.)

Literature and meaning

The above suggestions concerned introducing children to analysis of metaphors taken from the context of the narratives of which they formed a part. This kind of exercise is particularly useful if integrated within a wider scheme of work which has as its aim the introduction of children to narratives which are potentially rich in layers of meaning. Teaching which has this aim as its focus, of course, ought not to be restricted to Religious Education, and this point illustrates the inadvisability of teaching 'in boxes', as it were. Although teachers need to be quite clear concerning what it is they are attempting to teach, the aims and objectives can be addressed through a variety of subjects.

It is here that the use of literature and religious narratives resemble each other in their effect on the development of thought and understanding. The following comments of Bettelheim concerning the psychological value of traditional fairy tales is important for religious material, too:

> The conscious and unconscious associations which fairy tales evoke in the mind of the listener depend on his general frame of reference and his personal preoccupations. Hence, religious persons will find in them much of importance.
>
> (Bettelheim, 1991, 13)

However, the teacher needs to be able to respond appropriately to the almost inevitable question 'But is it true?' If events can be anchored in history, they undoubtedly seem to be more attractive and persuasive than those that appear to be more fantastical (see Chapter 5 for discussion on this). However, pupils can be led towards the interesting idea that some narratives embody insights which are based on life's experiences and which are worthy of consideration when one is faced with any similar dilemma. They have their own unique status.

In Box 3.4 a story is suggested which presents dilemmas to both pupils and their teacher, although of different types! The dilemma for the teacher is whether or not to try to explain the various implications of the events described for one's own life, or whether simply to tell the story to the children and discuss with them elements that relate to its literal

interpretation only. The dilemma for the children is presented at the end
of the story.

Box 3.4 Buddhist narrative: 'The Villagers and the Tiger'

The villagers in a tiny village in India were terrified of a big tiger
which came prowling around their village each evening. The trouble
was the tiger was very hungry, starving in fact, and it was desperate
to find some food. The people were afraid of ending up inside the
tiger's stomach!

At last the leader of the village called a meeting of all the people.
The night before many children had been terrified by the snarls of the
tiger as it made its way past their huts, sniffing here and there for bits
of food. One boy described how its eyes had glowed like lamps in the
darkness. He had begun to cry, and his sobs had awoken his litter
sister who had begun to cry too. Someone else described how the
tiger had started jumping up at the windows of her hut. She had
been afraid that it would knock the wall down! A man described
how he had kept his dagger ready by his bedside. He would have
been quite ready to tackle the tiger in a battle to the death had it
threatened either his family or himself.

The question, of course, was what should the villagers do?
Suddenly a stranger joined the meeting, a quiet man who asked if he
could listen to the discussion. He sat deep in thought as the people of
the village discussed their problem. Because they could not arrive at
a decision, the stranger asked if he could offer some advice.

'God made the tiger, just as he made you', said the man. 'The tiger
needs food just as you do. I think the village should provide food for
the tiger, and keep out of its way, rather than seek to destroy it'.

Some of the people agreed with the stranger, but there were others
who did not. They argued that it was better to get rid of the dangerous beast once and for all.

• *What do you think the village people should have done?*

Discussion

First let us examine the children's task: to discuss what the villagers should
have done. This story represents a dilemma for people which has never
been satisfactorily resolved. The Buddha believed that the tiger should
have been avoided, that is, not attacked or provoked unnecessarily.

However, Karl Marx believed that the tiger should have been destroyed because the villagers were entitled to defend themselves. Discussion with the children could raise the following points:

- Why should the tiger be attacked, even killed, just because it was hungry? We have all felt hunger at some time or another and should sympathise with it.
- If the people of the village kept out of the tiger's way, as Buddha suggested, it would probably move away to somewhere where food was available.
- If the people attacked and killed the tiger, what would the actual killing of the animal be likely to do to them as people?
- If the tiger killed animals belonging to the villagers, or even some of the villagers themselves, would that justify its own killing?

The dilemma of the teacher is whether to help the children perceive other, deeper, implications of the story – that is, to probe below and beyond its literal level. This would depend to a large extent on the individuals being taught. It would probably be wise to consider the following:

- the possibility of discussion with some individuals or groups who initiated discussion;
- alluding to the story on later occasions, for example, when telling the children about St George and the Dragon;
- leaving the children to dwell on the implications of the story in their own time and in ways natural to them;
- developing a scheme of work on conservation issues, bearing in mind that tigers do not become man-eaters unless they have learned to fear people. This theme would include material on the responsibility of people for the stewardship of the earth (see Ashton, 1994b for further ideas).

The overall purpose of introducing the children to the story would be to encourage them to think in depth around a problem, and to become aware of the varied implications of decision-making.

At deeper levels, of course, the tiger story can be understood as being about the human condition: pacifism or direct action; striking back at an assailant or 'turning the other cheek'; whether it is best to defeat evil by destruction or attempting to bring good from evil.

Creating an ethos for philosophical/religious thinking

The essence of being able to appreciate and work with language in multiple layers of meaning depends, to a great extent, on early influences during childhood. There can be little doubt that richness of experiences does much to encourage thought in depth by motivating curiosity, sensitivity and sympathy to all manner of phenomena. For example, this is how the sister of Sir Edward Elgar described how she and her brother were encouraged to appreciate the natural world:

> We were told never to *dare* destroy what we could not give – that was, the life – ever again. There is a humanity in every flower and blade of grass. We were encouraged to go out in all weather during the whole of the year. Although we honestly loved the winter we welcomed the beautiful time of spring: the singing birds had come, hedge and heath, fields and forests were offering their gifts of flowers as a pledge that winter was over.
>
> (Allison, 1994, 11)

The sensitivity which these earliest experiences encouraged no doubt contributed enormously to the work of the great composer. Small children are particularly aware of minute details of their surroundings and their reflections on them do much to influence their outlook on life generally. Stephen, a nine year old whom I once taught, described an experience he had undergone as a five year old playing hide and seek:

> I can remember that Tony was the catcher. He closed his eyes and counted to twenty to give us time to hide. We raced off. I wondered where to go, and saw some long grass at the edge of the field. I threw myself down among it, and lay there quietly. It was so quiet and still. I looked at the brown stems of the long grass, poking up from the earth and noticed a tiny spider crawling over the wet soil. There was a funny smell there – damp, and it made me want to cough. I lay there hiding for about quarter of an hour and Tony did not find me. I remember tracing the leaves of some weeds with my finger, thinking what a lovely pattern they made, and then I jumped up to show myself. The others had given up looking for me and had gone in for their tea.

Many children will describe similar experiences if encouraged and given time to do so. Kerry wrote the following lines about a school outing she remembered going on 'when I was in the infants':

> We went to the beach. I remember picking up a handful of sand and saying to the teacher 'I wonder how many little bits of sand I'm holding?' She pointed to the beach and said 'That's nothing! How many grains of sand do you think will be on this whole beach?' I said 'EHHH!' and ran to play with my friends. Some times I think about that when I am trying to get to sleep and can't.

41

School outings provide marvellous opportunities for encouraging children to engage in this type of thought, but it can be developed from the simplest observations. For example, five year old Allan was amazed when he viewed some grains of sand through a microscope for the first time. He exclaimed 'But it's like rocks!' The teacher was quick to point out it *was* rocks – tiny pieces of rock which had been broken up by the sea, wind and rain. As Allan went on to say, 'My eyes told me a lie!'

A student, Christine, told how she helped her class of five year olds make glasses for themselves, using different coloured pieces of acetate for the lenses. She said the children exclaimed in astonishment at how the different colours altered their view on the world. As she herself wrote:

> As the children were looking at a red or green world, I explained that the way in which each of us sees things is personal to us and how someone looking at the same thing might see it in an entirely different way to us, like looking through the different coloured lenses.

Christine explained that these children had an extremely limited experience of Religious Education. As she pointed out, 'I had felt it necessary to start with this "implicit" approach to religion'. Her aim had been to set a foundation, as it were, from which reflective thought could be stimulated. Her work with the class continued by examining the use of light in festivals – not coloured light this time, but candlelight and its religious significance (see Chapter 9, pp. 111–20 for further discussion of this theme).

Box 3.5 sets out a lesson plan concerning how a theme on 'Good and Evil' could be developed with Reception or Year 1 pupils, using the Walt Disney video (or story) of Snow White and the Seven Dwarfs.

Box 3.5 Lesson plan for Reception/Year 1: Good and Evil in the story of 'Snow White and the Seven Dwarfs'

Subject: Religious Education
Class: Reception or Year 1
Duration: 30 min.

Objectives:
1   To provide opportunities for the children to learn to distinguish good from bad (or evil).
2   To encourage in-depth thought and discussion about the children's reactions to what they have heard/seen.

Method: Either read the part of the story of 'Snow White' when the wicked Queen's servant cannot bring himself to kill her,

---

her run through the forest and discovery of the little house, or let the children watch an extract from the video which shows Snow White's forest run, the horrors of the wood and the way in which the animals came to her rescue.

Part 1   Children to either watch the video or listen to the story. Teacher to note any exclamations or other reactions for follow-up work.

Part 2   Opportunities provided for children to recount their feelings about the experience.

Part 3   Class work on a large wall-frieze of the forest scene. One group to produce a large 'Snow White', others to produce various animals and birds. Teacher could paint a 'background' for the children's work. Children to be given freedom to suggest other things they would like to include. Teacher to circulate among working groups, reinforcing the discussion developed in Section 2.

Part 4   The frieze to be used in later lessons as a 'visual aid' for writing and reading activities. Teacher will label items on the frieze appropriately.

Follow-up Many possibilities. A theme on 'Light and Darkness' could be developed; vocabulary work on good words to describe Snow White's experience. The class could produce a 'Snow White' album, filled with pictures, drawings and any other ideas stimulated by the work developed.

Through careful development of the story of 'Snow White', very young children can be introduced to the notion of good and evil being in conflict and encouraged to make their own judgements, according to the evidence provided, on which is the better position! Integrated with work of this kind can be more explicitly religious material, for example, 'Daniel in the Lion's Den', introducing the idea that perhaps what we call 'God' can be matched with 'good', and the converse position.

Conclusion

Teaching in Religious Education which develops in this way is so closely associated with levels of meaning in language that the two become inseparable. Sensitivity and thoughtfulness can be encouraged and developed through careful teaching, especially in language development, and supported by work in other subjects, especially in the arts. Metaphor offers an exciting medium through which this reflective thought can be deepened by the consideration of religious insights.

A third dimension to teaching of this kind is conceptual development, whereby pupils are encouraged to examine their assumptions as their ideas develop. It is to this that we shall turn in the next chapter.

4

DEVELOPING RELIGIOUS CONCEPTS

Introduction

As long ago as 1967 (see Plowden, 1967) the recommendation was made that conceptual development in Religious Education was the likely way in which the subject would move forward, leaving behind the days of confessionalism and the 'give them the facts of religion' approach to the subject. However, over thirty years later there is little evidence that this vision has ever been satisfactorily approached, never mind achieved. There are several reasons for this, not least of all the research work of Goldman (1964, 1965) who, as mentioned earlier (p. 13, 34) argued that children below the age of about twelve years were unable to think 'religiously'.

However, with the growth of understanding concerning how young children reflect on experience, question and develop conceptually, there is now every reason to believe that their thinking about religion can be helped to develop in ways similar to their work in, for example, Mathematics, Science or History. This chapter, therefore, provides ideas on how conceptual development could be achieved in Religious Education. I shall begin, however, with an investigation into the nature of concepts.

The development of concepts: the case of God

Concepts are mental structures which help us to assimilate experiences and information, and to formulate, as a result, values, theories and opinions which may, or may not, be based on informed judgement. It is the role of education to encourage pupils to think for themselves and to redefine the contents of these conceptual structures as they gain more experience of life in its many facets. However, how can these conceptual structures be understood? Obviously, if teachers are in the business of developing them, they will need to have some idea of how they can be perceived.

Cooper (1985, 27) likened concepts to maps, in the case of history to chronological maps which are 'constantly changing as new information and new processes are added'. This is helpful, particularly in that the metaphor expresses a flexibility that is sensitive to new insights and information and the necessity of refining and developing one's perceptions as greater understanding develops. Maps are never static: they are constantly being redrawn to accommodate new discoveries and changes, and use a variety of signs and symbols which are tangible and readily accessible. However, mind maps are not quite the same, for obvious reasons.

Another way of envisaging concepts is to think of them as networks, or associations of ideas, which are largely metaphorical in the way in which they are constructed. For example, here is what a six year old told me about God and heaven. It should be noted that the child was a Muslim:

> God is very kind to people. You go up to heaven when you die. Heaven is a lovely place. Heaven is in the sky. It is where people go when they die if they are old. Heaven is in the clouds and it is God's home. My mam's dad died. He is up in heaven now. God has a long white beard.

On asking him in detail why he thought these things, the following points became apparent:

1   Heaven is thought as being in the sky because people always talk about going 'up' to it. Spatial orientation is closely connected with the word 'up', and to rise from earth usually infers to pass towards the clouds. The conventional metaphor 'up', however, does not necessarily have to be used in this way (see Box 4.1 below). The assumption in all its respects receives reinforcement from society generally, particularly through religious paintings, drawings and symbolism (see pp. 31–2).

2   The natural tendency, when hearing the word 'God', is to relate it to something tangible. As shown above, God becomes envisaged as a man whose bodily characteristics become prominent rather than personality attributes; thus heaven becomes, logically, his 'home'.

3   When children face experiences of bereavement, especially of those close to them, it is not easy to provide comfort. They will ask 'where has grandfather gone?', for example. An easy way is to say 'he has gone to heaven to be with God', or something similar. Therefore, the spatial aspects of the concepts seem to hold together, at least at this particularly early time of development. However, this kind of response merely reinforces inadequate conceptual development which is not true to any of the world's great religions.

Here is a further example of crude anthropomorphism, this time recorded during a conversation between a teacher and a five year old:

CHILD: Who is Jesus?
TEACHER: Jesus is God's son.
CHILD: Well, when Jesus was little, did God take him to the park?
TEACHER: How do you mean?
CHILD: My daddy won't take me to the park. He never has time.
Would God have bought Jesus new trainers when he wanted them?
TEACHER: Jesus would have to pray for things he wanted, just as we do.

I am most grateful to the teacher who allowed me to sit in on this conversation. Various points arise from it, which are helpful in understanding how the child is attempting to conceptualise his notions of both God and Jesus' 'sonship' which, of course, is a metaphorical way of expressing Jesus' closeness and spiritually to God.

- The child conceptualises both 'God' and 'Jesus' as male figures, Jesus being literally God's son.
- He attempts to identify his own relationship with his father through what he imagines Jesus' might have been. Therefore, we see his concerns – about playing in the park, wanting new trainers, with the demands Jesus, as God's (literal) son, might have made. Perhaps he is trying to justify his demands, in his own mind.
- Unfortunately, the final response of the teacher is likely to reinforce another notion of God – that he could be a kind of 'slot machine'! Therefore, one has only to pray for what one desires, and one is sure to get it. However, as life's experience shows, things do not work that way at all.

Children will apply these de-religionised concepts to all manner of experiences which they undergo. For example, when a friend of mine had to have his dog destroyed for sheep-killing, his six-year-old son said during tea: 'Will Goldie jump up at Jesus when he gets to Heaven?'
A particularly worrying aspect of the problem was summed up by John Hull (1986, 60):

It is from detheologised adults that young children pick up such clichés (these are little more than verbalisms). God is male, is old, looks after us, makes flowers grow, and that we go to be with Jesus when we die, etc. What we find in this repertoire of child-like religiosity is very little intrinsic to childhood, but a great deal which indicates the puerilization of adult religious life.

The findings of Petrovich (1989) make another very important point. Working with children as young as three and four, she found they were able to distinguish between man-made and natural objects, citing God, or an unknown power, as creator of the latter. On further questioning, she discovered very few of her informants thought of this God or power as a man, rather as a person without a body or something like air or gas. Some of the children could not give an answer whilst others felt that there was no God. These concepts were quite sophisticated. However, if she began conversing with the children about 'God' as a word which they had learned, most of them said it referred to a man.

Her conclusions – that children learn from adults to think in crude anthropomorphic terms – were polarised by those of Piaget (1930), who argued that such concepts were natural to childhood. If the findings of Petrovich are enlightening for teachers' understanding of how children think and conceptualise in religion, the way forward is clear:

1   Children need to be helped by programmes of study in Religious Education to use and interpret a variety of metaphors of God, as used through the great world religions.
2   Work in Religious Education becomes increasingly interrelated with work carried out to increase literacy, both in thinking, verbal expression and the use of written language. Metaphor is a central component of this, and lessons could focus, from the early years, on helping children explore the spoken and written word on many levels of meaning.

However, it seems to be true that many adults are unable to offer their children anything better because their own education has failed to educate in religious thinking! As many undergraduate students have admitted to me, they believe subjects like mathematics, science and history are much easier to teach because there is something tangible which they feel able to transmit to children, whether it is figures, physical laws or documentary evidence. However, they often have argued that in religion there seems to be a lack of anything definite which can be taught. Again evidence of the apparent 'fact' and 'opinion' division is revealed! And yet the reality of good and evil in the world is very obvious, as a reading of the daily newspapers makes very clear. It is here that teachers could find a wealth of material to help pupils cope with their own developing concepts and the values which form as a result of experience and reflection.

Box 4.1 provides examples of how the great world religions conceptualise 'God', whichever title is used, for example, Allah, Jehovah or Brahman. It is suggested that readers might find the list helpful when faced with the task of selecting an appropriate concept for development in the classroom (see Boxes 4.2 and 4.3 for a development of this).

Box 4.1 Concepts of God in the world religions

God is being	Has existence rather than non-existence Note: 'being' does not refer to a supernatural being!
God is truth	Is concerned with honesty, knowledge and trustworthiness
God is love	Is filled with sympathy and compassion for the human condition
God is goodness	Is concerned with morality and living that is positive, rather than negative
God is life-giving	Is independent of other sources of life
God is immanent	Is present in the world
God is transcendent	Is within, and yet beyond, everything that exists
God is supreme	Is greater than anything that can be imagined
God is holy	Is concerned with rightness and goodness
God is all-knowing	Has unlimited knowledge
God is omnipotent	Has unlimited power
God is creator	Is responsible for the universe and the world
God is indescribable	Cannot be described in word, picture, music or any medium
God is incomprehensible	Is beyond the power of human reason and thought
God is immortal	Is unrestricted by physical ageing and death
God is infinite	Is not limited in any respect whatsoever
God is eternal	Is not confined to time
God is omnipresent	Is not confined to space
God is reality	Is not just a product of the human mind
God is spiritual	In contrast to physical
There is only one God	Not a multiple of gods and goddesses

It will be seen from the categories of God that crude anthropomorphism does not form a part of the insights which the great religions of the world hold *vis-à-vis* the nature and mystery of God. Teachers might find it helpful, when teaching concepts of God, to listen to the comments made by small children in respect of 'God' and refer to the above list for the concept which could usefully be developed by classroom work. Box 4.2 gives examples, drawn from classroom practice, whilst Box 4.3 gives suggestions of how work schemes could be developed.

Box 4.2 Children's comments about God: where to move next

- 'Will Goldie jump up at Jesus when he gets to heaven?'
- 'Heaven is where dead people live.'
- 'I prayed that my dog would get better but it died.'
- 'If God made the world, who made God?'

- 'Can I draw a picture of God?'
- 'Can God see me now?'

- God is omnipresent; God is love; God is spiritual
- God is spiritual; God is omnipresent
- God is love; God is all-knowing
- God is spiritual; God is omnipresent; God is eternal; God is infinite; God the Creator
- God is indescribable
- God is immanent; God is infinite

Teachers might find it useful to collect statements and questions of this kind which are made by children in their classes, classify them against the ways of understanding what religions mean by 'God', and use the results to develop lesson materials, or structures for discussion. Here are a few examples of what could be done.

Box 4.3 Lesson planning – concepts of God and pupils' comments and questions

Concept of God to develop	Suggestions for lesson content
God as creator	Aim to discourage 'All Things Bright and Beautiful' images. Instead, encourage children to question and reflect on the reality of the natural world. **Story**. A lady bought a bird-feeder, a little plastic tube which she filled with nuts and hung in a tree in her garden. Soon lots of little sparrows found it and began to cheep amongst themselves jumping for a place on the feeder and enjoying the peanuts. The lady was really enjoying the scene when there was a sudden swishing noise, a thump, and the sparrows

---

flew off in terror – that is, except for one. This little bird had been caught in the claws of a big bird of prey, a sparrow-hawk. To the lady's horror, the sparrow-hawk perched in the tree with the little sparrow's body in its claws and began to eat it. The chirping sparrows were silent: there was horror and sadness in the garden, but the hawk had found some food.

Questions for pupils to consider:
- If God makes everything, why should a bird like a sparrow-hawk be made which kills and eats other birds?
- If the sparrow-hawk did not catch other birds, it would starve to death. Killing is its natural way of life. In a way, the little sparrow sacrificed its life to feed the bigger bird. That is what nature is like.
- Why is it that something so beautiful (like the sparrow-hawk) can sometimes seem to be very cruel? Can the children suggest other examples (e.g. spiders' webs, insect-eating plants (sundew), sea-anemone)?
- Do humans sometimes behave like the sparrow-hawk? What could 'Jean is a sparrow-hawk' mean?

God is omnipresent

Possible development of child's statement 'Heaven is up in the clouds, in the sky'.

TEACHER: Why do you think it's in the sky?

CHILD: Because if you keep going up you reach the sky.

TEACHER: Soon you will be going into Mrs Smith's class – you sometimes say 'I'll be going up after the holidays', don't you?

CHILD: Yes.

TEACHER: Do you mean you will be going up into the sky in her class?

CHILD: No! No! We will just change rooms.

TEACHER: Why do you say you will be going up, then?

CHILD: Er, I don't know!

TEACHER: Up can mean to go higher, but it can also mean something better, or harder (more difficult).

CHILD: Is heaven better, or harder, then?

Concept of God to develop	Suggestions for lesson content
	TEACHER: Many people say that; that heaven is a word that means 'better' or 'the next part', like Mrs Smith's class, but not up in the sky!
God is love/ all-knowing	Child complains that she prayed for a fine day for her school trip, but it rained. She reckons God did not answer her prayers.
	TEACHER: When you ask you dad for sweets, does he always buy them for you? CHILD: Sometimes, but not always because they are bad for my teeth! TEACHER: So your dad sometimes says you cannot have what you want? CHILD: Yes. TEACHER: Do you think that could be because he loves you and knows what is best for you? CHILD: Yes. TEACHER: Well, perhaps that could be one of the ways in which God is like a good father!
God is Spirit	Child asks what 'spirit' means. Teacher could suggest it is a bit like energy: if our torch does not have a battery, it will not light. It needs energy. If our television set is not plugged in, it will not work. It needs energy. People say God is a bit like energy: God's spirit is sometimes called 'energy' – something like electricity, or a battery, or the wind. God's energy makes good things happen.

The above are examples, not necessarily of lessons, but of incidental work with children which could develop from a casual comment which reveals a need for development of a certain type of religious concept. The aim is to help children move beyond crude anthropomorphisms and to begin to consider real theological insights and ideas for themselves by relating them to their own thoughts and questions.

Further concepts for development in the Early Years

There are several other religious concepts which are appropriate for development with Early Years children – that is, the process of development can be started during the first three years of school, in the hope that it will encourage further reflection throughout life. Given below are discussions of these concepts, with ideas for classroom work.

God is known by many names

Because of the indescribable nature of the deity which transcends, or lies beyond, the capacity of direct depiction through either thought, word, image or any other media, it is recognised by all the great religions of the world that many names, images or metaphors are needed in order to communicate insights. These names, images and metaphors act as signposts, as it were, pointing the way towards understanding, but they should not be considered as destinations: rather, they are guides, or pointers which indicate something of the enormity to which they lead.

In Hinduism, for example, Brahman is the ultimate or absolute, which defies all attempts at definition. Brahman is neutral and impersonal, comprising the origin, cause and foundation for all existence. The essence of Brahman is pure being [*at*], pure intelligence [*cit*] and pure delight [*ananda*]. Brahman is the unknowable one, and can only be considered through personal deities. Therefore, Brahman is manifested in a variety of forms which signify cosmic and natural forces. Although Hindu communities may each worship different manifestations of Brahman, they are aspects of the one reality, ways of approaching the ultimate reality. Examples include:

Indra: the god of the thunderbolt who was able to suppress the dragon that tried to prevent the flow of life-giving waters

Agni: the god of fire and sacrifice, who unites heaven, earth and the atmosphere in between

Vishnu: the great preserver, symbol of divine love

Lakshmi: Vishnu's female counterpart, symbolic of beauty and good fortune.

In Islam, Allah is regarded as having three thousand names, none of which is adequate to express precisely what Allah is. Ninety-nine of these names are to be found in the Qur'an, but the greatest name of all has been hidden by Allah. In popular opinion, the one-hundredth name is said to have been revealed only to the camel, which will not disclose it! It is described as follows:

He who is worshipped by you is One God, there is no god but Him, the Compassionate and Beneficent (Sura II, 163); also in the first part of Sura Ali Imran, Alif Lam Mim – Allah, there is no god but Him, the Alive, the Self-Subsisting.

(Friedlander, 1993, 8)

In Judaism, the indescribable nature of the deity is communicated through various names which have emerged throughout different periods of Jewish history as new insights developed. In the original Hebrew of the Christian Old Testament, for example, in the Creation narrative, God is referred to as Elohim, the Divine, the Ultimate Spiritual Reality. However, scholars argue that YHWH refers to the name which the Hebrew people believed Elohim revealed to Moses. YHWH means I THAT AM – that is, Being.

As discussed above, the most prevalent metaphor of God in Christianity is 'father', and because of the unfortunate misunderstandings that accompany its use, very careful teaching is needed to correct and modify crude anthropomorphisms. This can be done by introducing pupils to other metaphors of God which abound through Christian scripture, for example

Light:	God is the opposite of darkness: growing enlightenment brings increased understanding and wisdom.
Good Shepherd:	God cares for his creation as a good shepherd cares for his flock.
A Rock:	God is everlasting and dependable.

Box 4.4 provides ideas on how to help children begin to understand the concept of 'One God, Many Names'.

Box 4.4 Introducing the concept of 'One God, Many Names'

Children need to be introduced to the idea that one thing, or person, can be called a variety of names, according to insights of different people, relationships and roles. The following are ideas on how this could be done, leading to work on the concept of God having many names and forms, yet remaining One.

Lesson 1: Thinking about the cuckoo-pint wild flower

- Either show the children a picture of cuckoo-pint flowers, or even better, produce a specimen.
- Children could draw or paint the flower.

- Tell the children the plant has a lot of names.

- Names given to cuckoo-pint include

  - Lords and Ladies
  - Jack in the Pulpit
  - Devils and Angels
  - Soldier in a Sentry Box.

- Make the point that, although the flower has many names, they do not change the plant. Each name gives us a new idea about it.

- Children could suggest names, with reasons, and discuss in class.

- Children could decide which names they think are most suitable.

- Discuss the names with the children. Can they think of any better ones? Can they suggest why people thought of these names in the past?

- Can the children suggest anything else which has more than one name? Do the names help us understand it in different ways?

Story

Long, long ago some nuns came to England from France and they brought with them some cuckoo-pint plants. A little later, some monks from Ely Cathedral stole the body of a saint, Withburga, from a nearby town, Dereham. They were taking the body down the river, back to Ely, when they felt so tired they had to stop for rest. Nuns who lived nearby ran down to the river, and because they had loved the saint so much, they threw cuckoo-pint flowers on to the body.

Some of the flowers fell into the water, and they immediately grew roots. Soon cuckoo-pint flowers covered all the banks of the river – a miracle seemed to have taken place. Even more astonishing was that in the night a mysterious glow seemed to come from the flowers, as though they were trying to show the saint had special powers.

In the last century, hundreds of years later, workmen from Ireland noticed the strange light given by the pollen of the flowers and called them 'Fairy Lamps'.

(*Note*: this story could be used as an Introduction to a study of the symbols Light and Darkness; see Chapter 12.)

Lesson 2: Who is my granny?

Tell the children that Peter had noticed different people call his granny different names. This is what he had heard:

His father called her .... Mother
His mother called her .... Mil (mother-in-law)
His grandfather called her .... Mabel
His friend Michael called her .... Doctor Jones
A classmate, Susan, called her .... Brown Owl
His next-door neighbour called her .... Mrs Jones

Peter was puzzled, so he asked his dad about it. His dad laughed, and lifted him on to his knee. 'It's like this', he explained, 'your granny is my mother, but she is your mum's mother-in-law, shortened to Mil. But she is your grandfather's wife, so he calls her Mabel, her Christian name. Your granny is Michael's doctor, so when he feels ill he goes to her for help and calls her Doctor. But your granny runs a Brownie Pack, and the girls who are in the Pack call her Brown Owl, the name Pack Leaders have. Our neighbour just calls her Mrs Jones, because she does not know anything about all the other things she does.'

Peter said, 'But she is still my granny, isn't she – it doesn't matter what people call her!'

'Yes', said his dad, 'and she is still my mother!'

(Note: Make the point that people throughout the world call God by different names, but all believe there is only one God, no matter what names and titles are used.)

Popular RE themes in the Early Years and concepts of God

Two well-known narratives from the Judaic tradition which form a part of Early Years teaching in many schools are The Creation and The Great Flood (or Noah's Ark). Both of these traditions offer many important opportunities for helping children develop their concepts of God, but if not handled carefully could well have the opposite effect and reinforce, or even introduce, crude anthropomorphisms!

Box 4.5 suggests ideas for using the narratives to enable children to think about God in ways that could provide a foundation for more conceptual work, particularly if combined with the ideas on how to introduce metaphor in language to children suggested earlier (Chapter 3).

Box 4.5 Creation and Flood: developing concepts of God

Lesson 1: The Creation

The Creation narrative (Genesis 1, vv. 1–31; 2, v. 1–4) can be used to introduce children to the idea of God as Creator by discussing with them the first five verses from Genesis:

> In the beginning God created the heaven and the earth. And the earth was without shape, and empty; and darkness was upon the face of the deep. And the spirit of God moved upon the face of the waters. And God said, 'Let there be light': and there was light. And God saw the light, that it was good: and God divided the light from the darkness. And God called the light Day, and the Darkness he called Night. And the evening and the morning were the first day.

This narrative, written in ancient times, was never intended to be a scientific account of Creation, although the sequencing of events, fascinatingly, does correspond to a scientific structure. Rather, it can be understood as a great hymn, written in celebration of the fact that there is something, rather than nothing.

It is therefore suggested that children could enjoy reciting some of the verses: because they are wonderfully poetic, they are quite easily remembered.

It is not helpful to present this narrative as a contrasting view to that of science: rather it is complementary, wondering at the marvels of the natural world, and all it came to mean for Creation. The following points could be raised and discussed with the children:

- That in the beginning, God created something from nothing. Give the children a few minutes to sit with closed eyes and to think about this. Could they make something from absolutely nothing?
- 'The Spirit of God moved upon the face of the waters': 'spirit', or in Hebrew, *ruach*, means breath, power, energy, the spirit or authority of God. Again, the point could be made that one word can have many meanings.
- 'God said, "Let there be light".' This can mean God is concerned with all positive things which light can symbolise (see Chapter 9 for further ideas for lessons).

It is important to discuss with the children how the narrative goes on to tell us God separated 'the firmament' (i.e. dry land) from 'the waters'. A dome, or arch, was envisaged as holding the waters back. These were pictured as being something like shutters which opened when it rained. Of course, the people knew they were using 'picture language' – they would be able to see, as we do now, that rain really comes from the clouds!

What this poem is maintaining is that:

- God (Elohim) was responsible for creating all that is;
- Creation took place through the action of power, or the authority of God – i.e. through Elohim's breath, or spirit;
- God was pleased with what had been achieved;
- water symbolised potential chaos, whilst dry land symbolised order (i.e. 'light'). Yet both are necessary for the continuation of life.

Activities

These could involve drawing and painting in order to reinforce the ideas introduced during discussion, recitation of selected verses and perhaps the production of a classroom frieze.

Lesson 2: The Great Flood or Noah's Ark

The story of Noah (Genesis 6, vv. 5–9; v. 17) tells how God, becoming dissatisfied with how the created world had developed, decided to rid the earth of everything that was evil by causing a great flood. The story was probably passed on orally for centuries before being written down on papyrus; no doubt small changes were made each time the story was retold. Different traditions seem to have been brought together in the Biblical narrative. The earliest written tradition was probably recorded around 10 BCE, but by the third century BCE the traditions became combined, producing the narrative we now have.

There are many children's versions of this narrative, the main points of which are summarised below:

God saw the wickedness of man, and was sorry he had made people on earth. The Lord said, 'I will destroy what I have created, both man, and beast and the creeping thing, and the fowls of the air'; but Noah was recognised by God as being good.

God then instructed Noah to build a great ark. Into it went all Noah's family, and two of every beast and fowl, male and female, to keep the seed on the earth. After seven days the waters of the flood were upon the earth. All the fountains of the deep were broken up, and the windows of heaven were opened. And all that lived was destroyed from the earth. Only Noah, and they that were with him, remained alive, safe in the ark.

After forty days, Noah opened the window of the ark and sent out a raven which flew back and forth until the waters had dried; he also sent out a dove, but it found 'no rest for the sole of her foot'. Noah took her back into the ark, but after seven days it returned with an olive branch, in leaf; Noah knew the waters had abated. At length, God told Noah to leave the ark, with his family, so a new start could be made. The good would once again inhabit the earth. God set his bow in the sky as a promise made to Noah that never again would the waters of chaos flood the earth.

Following a reading of this narrative with the children, discussion could usefully focus around the following important points:

- *God was concerned with goodness* – See Box 4.2. (It is sometimes maintained that young children are likely to become upset at the thought of the drowning animals, but there is no evidence from classrooms to support this assertion. On the other hand, children are fascinated by the idea of two of every kind of creature finding safety in the ark.)
- *When the flood began, the waters of chaos, separated by God during creation, came together again.* This was because God wished to destroy evil, and maintain good.
- *Is the story true?* Young children are very likely to ask this question. There are many layers of meaning according to which this story can be understood. Certainly, there is archaeological evidence that some kind of serious flooding occurred (e.g. the findings of Sir Leonard Wooley digging at Ur in southern Mesopotamia found a layer of clay and water-borne debris 8 ft. thick. There were signs of human habitation both below and above these deposits.) Therefore, a great flood could well have happened in history.
- *It is certain the Hebrews were trying to say something about God.* Noah should be thought of as the good that exists in every person, rather than as a man who lived long ago. The story tells us 'goodness' will survive, but evil of every kind will be destroyed, because God is a God of goodness, love and power.

Activities

This narrative offers stimulating material for children's art work and drama. However, any such work should not stop there. Whilst discussing the story initially, and while circulating among children working on, say, a classroom display or frieze, the teacher should take every opportunity of discussing the above points in appropriate ways with them, principally that the story tells us about God's concern with truth, love and goodness.

Conclusion

Ideas were presented in this chapter to show how teaching in Religious Education can help develop children's concepts of God. This focus of teaching is an essential aspect of the subject, vital for understanding any of the world's religions.

More suggestions are contained in the following chapter, which looks at ways in which teachers could respond to the 'ultimate questions' which very young children inevitably ask.

5

CONVERSING WITH CHILDREN

Introduction

Young children regularly ask questions that can be extremely difficult to address. The purpose of this chapter is to identify different types of questions asked, the learning needs that underlie them, and the ways in which teachers can respond appropriately, both through conversation and schemes of work.

The depth of reflection of which the youngest child is capable should not be underestimated. Gareth Matthews has shown how Early Years children often show themselves capable of the type of philosophical thinking which underlies much of the theory expounded by the great masters (Matthews, 1980, 1984, 1994). This type of reflection underlies much of the insight of the world religions, and therefore provides another extremely valuable base from which teachers can develop important conversations and work with children.

Children's interest in metaphysical speculation

The questions which young children ask can be roughly classified in two broad categories. First, there are 'factual' questions, such as 'Please, may I play in the garden?' or 'Please, may I have another sweet?' These questions require a straight answer which is equally factual – usually 'yes' or 'no'.

However, as all parents recognise, there is a second category of questions which is much harder to deal with; these are often called 'ultimate questions'. Between these two extremes – 'factual' and 'ultimate' questions – there is a whole continuum of questions and comments which young children regularly raise. How teachers deal with them will influence responses to specifically religious ones, that is by listening, responding in depth, encouraging a reply from the child so that conversation can happen through opening up fresh ways of thinking about issues. it is very important that teachers should identify 'ultimate questions' and analyse them in order to make assessments of how the child is thinking, what clues the question provides for what could be appropriate teaching material to help the child move forward in his/her reflection, and lastly how the question could influence the content of future lesson planning. As indicated in the previous two chapters, it is vitally important that children's curiosity and thinking should not encounter a 'stone wall' which is insurmountable. The results of this all too common failure on the part of education to take children's questions seriously are revealed in the crude anthropomorphisms and de-religionised view of reality examined earlier (pp. 46–8).

The importance of this for education has been stressed by Petrovich (1988). As stated earlier (pp. 47–8), she showed how young children will transcend the empirical field and engage in metaphysical speculation about natural objects, life, death and suffering. Dewey too (1910, 65) warned against accepting notions that 'childhood is almost entirely unreflective ... a period of mere sensory, motor and memory developments, while adolescence suddenly brings the manifestation of thought and reason.'

Nor should this capacity and interest in metaphysical speculation be ignored or stifled on the grounds that it is 'unscientific' (see discussion on this in Chapter 1). Rather, the creative, positive aspects of the kind of thought which leads to 'ultimate questioning' is an important aspect of what it means to be human, and is invaluable for the classroom teacher (Ashton, 1993a). How, nevertheless, can it be addressed in ways that are educational and open to free enquiry?

Identification and analysis of ultimate questions

As mentioned above, ultimate questions comprise queries about philosophical and religious questions to which simple answers are inadequate. Teachers need to be mindful when conversing with pupils on these issues that children need to learn that we do not have answers to all the questions that arise from our experiences of life; indeed, why should we presume to be entitled to such insights? This can be a very difficult lesson for children to learn, as their questioning style is characterised by a desire for sharp, quick answers.

As pointed out by Brenda Watson (1987, 212), teachers are faced with a very responsible task, which is 'to be able at a second's notice to turn a chance remark into valuable theological, philosophical and scientific education'. This means that, instead of handing children 'answers on a plate' (which is what they probably have learned to expect and receive), opportunities should be seized to encourage their own thinking to broaden and deepen. In Box 5.1 there is an example of one child's question which is fairly typical of Early Years pupils. Below are given various possible responses, both adequate and unhelpful. Readers might find it helpful to reflect on the likely effects on the child's future thinking of each given response.

Box 5.1 Responding to an 'ultimate question': which is the best way forward?

- *'Jasper, my puppy, was killed by a car last night. I left the garden gate open and he ran outside. Why did God let it happen?'* (Martin, a distraught six year old.)

Possible responses:
1   Never mind, perhaps your daddy will buy you another puppy at the pet-shop.
2   Jasper died because you were careless and left the gate open. It is your fault, not God's.
3   If Jasper was badly hurt, it's better he should have died. God probably knew that.
4   Perhaps God was talking with the angels in heaven and didn't see what was happening.
5   Death and suffering are very puzzling, but they might all be part of God's plan. We should just keep thinking about it.
6   What would you like to do this morning? Why not play in the Wendy House?
7   We don't know the answers to all the questions we ask. Life is a bit like a jigsaw puzzle: sometimes we don't have all the pieces or some pieces are lost. All we can do is learn. What is there about your puppy's life you would like to give thanks for? These good things are what we thank God for.

Discussion

The child's statement and question raise the following points:

- How far is it reasonable to blame God for the evil that happens? Could the role of God be more concerned with helping us to cope and learn from experience?
- In this particular instance, the child has a very hard lesson to learn, which is the necessity of ensuring one is careful that animals do not have opportunities to roam. If this lesson is learned effectively early on in life, important wisdom has been gained which extends far beyond the care of animals. A terribly sad misfortune can then be seen in a positive light, although much later.
- God is not like a puppet-master: we have much free choice and sometimes must take responsibility for what we do.

Of course, these points should not be spelt out to a distressed, small child. However, they do provide guidance as to how essential it is that children are trained, and reminded constantly, about the importance of taking responsibility for pets; particularly how a moment's inattention can have disastrous results.

Comments on the possible responses (Box 5.1)

1 Response (1) in Box 5.1 avoids the point at issue. Although such replies are often given to children, they are unhelpful for helping them think through the event. Indeed, to buy a replacement puppy would do much to increase irresponsibility, rather than learn from the sadness experienced. This is because children would be likely to receive the message that the puppy Jasper was just a commodity, as easily replaceable as a new pair of trainers, for example, rather than a living creature with feelings, individuality and vitality.

2 The negative tone of the second response in Box 5.1 is likely to reinforce the child's feelings of distress. Theologically, in addition, it does nothing to help develop the child's religious understanding. God is likely to be perceived as another disapproving adult who offers no consolation or comfort.

3 Again, the comment offers nothing to help the child develop his understanding of the incident, and is likely to add to his stress. Crude anthropomorphism is likely to be encouraged by suggesting God could 'know' in physical terms, without discussion of how the word 'know' is used in this context.

4 This comment (4) in Box 5.1 would do even more to encourage crude anthropomorphisms, not only of God but also of heaven and angels. It offers no scope whatsoever for furthering the child's personal reflections and theological understanding. It is also dangerous in that it suggests God to be irresponsible and distracted!

5 Some important ideas are suggested in the fifth response – that death and suffering are mysteries. However, to suggest they could be part of 'God's plan' would do little to foster the child's desire to know more about God. In addition, a 'stone wall' is erected because no help is given the child concerning *how* he 'could just keep thinking about it'. In what direction could his thoughts usefully travel, and to what end? The comment is vague, and sadly characteristic of advice often given to young children.

6 Avoidance of the question is the main thrust of this response. Clearly, the adult in question did not have any idea how to respond in positive ways.

7 Of all seven responses, the last one is, quite obviously, the most appropriate. It uses metaphor to good effect (e.g. 'life is a jigsaw puzzle'), which is creative and likely to help the child channel his reflections

more positively. The idea of the puppy's contribution to happiness during its short life hints that there could, after all, have been much that was positive, and that it is this for which we should give thanks. The point to be stressed is that the pleasure given by the puppy is characteristic of God, rather than the accident which led to its death. This is because religions teach God is responsible for, and supportive of, good (the point made in the discussion of the Noah's Ark narrative in Box 4.5). However, it is mistaken to suppose God to be a kind of gift-provider, who will respond to one's wishes without question. It is equally wrong to conceptualise God in terms of the slot-machine, as discussed earlier (p. 47).

Because of the way in which the world operates – that is, according to physical laws – life is not always beautiful and we do not always have our wishes granted. It is a fact that we all will die, for example, and sometimes in quite distressing ways. For example, the hunting and eating habits of the sparrow-hawk referred to earlier (see Box 4.3) are far from attractive, although the bird itself is majestic, even awesome in appearance, and skilled in its search for prey. A question which could be usefully put to children concerns God's activity in the world – would everything be horrible and distressing if it were not for the divine concern for what is good? That is why it is right to give thanks for good, and to attempt to overcome evil: the doctrine that lies at the heart of religions.

Just as it is vital that teachers should help children cope with negative experiences of life in their thinking about God, it is equally important that they should not receive encouragement to think of God in ways that simply reflect popular beliefs, and which are untrue to the doctrines of the world religions. An example of this is provided in Box 5.2.

Box 5.2 Responding to an 'ultimate question': 'did God answer my prayer?'

- *'I prayed hard last night for sunny weather for our trip today. God answered my prayers. Look at the sunshine.'* (Rebecca, six years old.)

Possible responses:
1 Do you really think God had anything to do with that? It was just that the wind blew the clouds the right way for the sun to shine.
2 Hurry up. It's time we left. Get your things – the bus won't wait for ever.
3 Well, God knew what you wanted and he said 'Yes', so you believe in him. If it had been raining would you have believed in him then?

---

4 Isn't it lovely when things go right for us. Why do you think the world is such an exciting, beautiful place. Keep thinking about it.

5 That is all wrong. There is no such thing as God.

6 Perhaps God did answer your prayer – I think so, but some people would just say you have been lucky.

7 You do chatter on. Look, here comes the bus. We must run.

Discussion

The subtle danger with the statement is that it could be all too easy to encourage the child to think of God as a kind of slot-machine – that in order to have your wishes granted, all one has to do is 'put in a prayer or two'. It is therefore necessary for the teacher, somehow, to maintain some balance between the child either rejecting the idea of God because the prayer was not answered in the affirmative, or developing the simplistic notion that prayers are only answered if one gets one's own way, and that God must, therefore, exist!

Comments on possible responses (Box 5.2)

1 The first response could be argued as being an example of initiation into secularism. It assumes God's non-existence and encourages a scientific view of causation at the expense of the theological.

2 Quite obviously, the second response evades the responsibility of helping the child move forward in her thinking about God. The message she is likely to receive, therefore, is that such questions as God and prayer do not really have any importance.

3 Some important points are actually made in this response, but it is unfortunate in its actual wording, which could be interpreted as a sneer. Perhaps readers could spend a little time rewording the response so that it would be non-threatening to the child, but helpful in suggesting other ways of reacting to the experience. After all, it is very likely that many of her prayers in the future would not be answered in the way desired.

4 The intention of the fourth comment is good, but the wording is vague and unlikely to be helpful in conceptual development. How should she think about it? A possible way forward could be to suggest that, on this occasion, perhaps God had granted her wishes, but if this had not happened, the answer could simply have been 'no'. Sometimes prayers are answered negatively, as can be shown by reading how Jesus prayed that God would 'take this cup from me' (that he would not suffer crucifixion). However, he had to go

through the suffering. This is an example of the mystery at the heart of religion.

5   Again, this comment avoids opening up discussion of the important issues which need to be educationally developed. It is also dogmatic in tone, and quite unhelpful for pointing a possible way forward, other than absolute denial of the child's particular notion.

6   The teacher could have developed this comment more fully, perhaps by telling the child why she believed God had answered her prayer. As it stands, it is vague.

7   Again, comment (7) is evasive, and like response (2) is likely to condition the child against taking religions insights and ideas seriously.

Theological points arising from the statements in Boxes 5.1/5.2

Here is an example of how a conversation could be developed with a child which introduces and reinforces important theological points that arise from the above.

CHILD: Did God make the world or was it just the Big Bang?

TEACHER: I like to think God and the Big Bang are really joined.

CHILD: How do you mean?

TEACHER: You asked me if the world started by the Big Bang or by God, didn't you?

CHILD: Yes. Which was it?

TEACHER: If you throw a ball and smash a window, what or who would be to blame?

CHILD: The ball would break the glass, but I'd be to blame if I threw the ball.

TEACHER: Exactly. So the cause of the broken glass would be you, and what you did it with would be the ball! I think the Big Bang is like the ball breaking the glass, and God something like you, because God caused the Big Bang to happen!

CHILD: Yes. The ball and me are different things, and the Big Bang and God are different, but really they are joined up.

TEACHER: That's about right! [At this point another child, who was listening, joins the conversation.]

CHILD 2: What about when we say our prayers? Does God listen and do anything?

TEACHER: Think about yourself praying. What might you be praying about?

CHILD 2: Well, what about asking God to make my grandma well. She is in hospital for an operation.

TEACHER: The thing is this – your grandmother is not just 'a body'. She is also a person with feelings and thoughts. So are the doctors and nurses who look after her. What kind of things could you ask God for in your prayers?

CHILD 2: I could ask God to help my grandma not to be worried – to help her trust the doctors and nurses. Then she might not be so worried and might not feel so ill.

TEACHER: That would be a good thing to pray for. That is a way people believe God helps when we ask in our prayers.

CHILD 1: What if your grandmother did not feel better though?

TEACHER: Sometimes our prayers are answered, but not in the way we ask. For example, Jesus prayed that he might not be killed on the cross, but God seemed to say 'no'. Feeling ill and suffering pain – things like that – are really a mystery. But we'll come back to it when we think about Jesus on the Cross [see pp. 72, 185–7]. We cannot hope to understand everything from our life on this earth – time and space are so huge!

CHILD 1: Yes, sometimes I close my eyes and think about space – but I just get cut off.

CHILD 2: My grandma always says you have to just trust God. She is going to when she is in hospital.

TEACHER: And you can help her by praying for her. Then she will know she has a lot of support and will feel better. That seems to be a way in which God's power works.

CHILD 1: I'm going to think more about this tonight and I'll ask you something else tomorrow!

TEACHER: Great! But don't think I can just give you all the answers you want! Often we have to keep thinking about things like this for a very long time!

Thinking through angels and haloes

It is not only the spoken and written word which can cause misunderstandings about religion. The same applies to many of the signs and symbols on which religions heavily depend in order to communicate many teachings and insights. Like metaphors, if taken literally they can eventually do much to diminish religious faith, but on uninformed grounds.

Whilst there are many teaching aids commercially produced, and of a good quality, they will not help children understand the significance of symbol in religious devotion and thought unless some very important teaching points are incorporated in programmes of study which avoid giving – or reinforcing – the notion that symbols merely 'stand for' something that is absent. In religion, symbols are much more than this. They point in particular ways to that which is present by drawing attention to it in vivid, unforgettable ways. It is because of this vividness that certain religious symbols will remain prominent in the minds and imaginations of young children.

For example, I remember how a colleague with responsibility for teaching five year olds told me about a class visit to the local Anglican parish church for the Harvest Festival Service, on which occasion the church had been beautifully decorated with produce donated by both the children and staff. On their return, she let the children draw what they had seen, with the intention of mounting the pictures of fruit and vegetables and using it as a visual aid in follow-up work on the theme of harvest.

However, when she collected in the drawings and paintings later to mount, she found herself faced not with apples, onions, flowers, cabbages and oranges, but with twenty-eight versions of the crucifixion! It had not been the harvest produce which had grasped the attention of most of the children, but the carving of Jesus on the cross above the rood screen! From a class of thirty children, only two had thought of drawing and colouring harvest produce! Undoubtedly this was because such everyday items as these proved to be very ordinary and lacking in excitement when such an arresting, unusual scene, comprising not only the crucifixion victims but figures standing in grief beneath them, angels and Roman soldiers, provided an alternative for young curious minds.

Here was an opportunity to 'plug into' the object of the children's fascination. In particular, it provided the chance to do some important work on religious symbolism, as described below.

• *'Miss, what are those yellow circles above people's heads?'*

The halo in Christian art is a symbol that arouses the interest of young children, and the above question is of a type regularly asked. What young children desire to know are the following:

1 Why people are shown with circles of light around their heads.
2 Why people today don't have light around their heads.

It is very important that from an early age children should be introduced to symbols in religion, and to learn that they are intended to signify a variety of religious truths. Quite simply, haloes are used by artists to show which people are particularly holy, or close in spirit to what religions mean by 'God'.

The problem with the questions in (1) and (2) above concern literalism. They reveal that the questioner is thinking that the people 'of long ago' – probably, although not necessarily, people who feature in Biblical material – developed a circle of light around their head. To tell them the halo shows 'they were very good' or that 'they were close to God' is unlikely to help them think beyond a literal level, because question (2) is almost certain to follow! Unless the children are helped to think beyond these literal levels, the misunderstandings inherent in them will undermine the possibility of their becoming informed about religion. Somehow the teacher must devise discussions and activities which help the children understand. Below are possible responses to the respective questions.

1   Haloes are painted by artists, or sculpted by sculptors, to show which people in the picture were holy, or who did all they could to live according to God's way. The artist could not write on the painting 'This person is close to God'! It is much better, and more interesting, to use a halo to show this. In a way, it is like a secret code which can be easily read by those who understand it.
2   No-one is likely to be found going around the streets or shops with a halo around their head! However, if someone was really special, and did everything to follow God's teachings, if an artist painted him/her at some time, it is possible that a halo would be painted around the person's head. That is what artists of the past did, too.

In Box 5.3 are some suggestions of activities which teachers could use to try to get these points across to children. Many in Year 1, and nearly all in Year 2, could be expected to grasp the above points.

Box 5.3 Learning to understand haloes: some activities

- Provide a variety of pictures of people with haloes and discuss.
- Point out to the children that the people with haloes were very close to God. The halo is what the artist uses to show this.
- Point out to the children the halo is made of light.

- Remind the children of characters from stories they know well. Which of them would they give haloes to?
- Discuss with the children some famous people from today, and provide pictures from the media.

- The children could discuss who the people are, and what the halo might mean.
- The children could be asked to suggest what, in our time, could qualify people for a halo.

- Can the children think of other ways whereby the artist could tell us which were good people?
- The children could do their own drawings of people with haloes.

- Children could cut out the figures to mount in a wall-book, if they thought they were good enough to qualify for a halo.

- *'Are there any angels now? I've never seen one!'*

The problem inherent in the above question bears similarities to the one concerning haloes. The speaker does not understand that angels can be understood symbolically, as well as literally. Again, if thinking does not gradually deepen beyond this surface level, the underlying literalism will gradually undermine the possibility that religion could offer guidance for one's own decision-making and values generally. This is because, if there aren't any angels, maybe there isn't a God either!

Young children, nor surprisingly, frequently confuse angels and fairies – both are usually shown with wings. If the confusion is not cleared up at an early stage of their education, it is likely to persist for many years, leading to the rejection of the religious truths expressed by the symbolism out of hand, and on uninformed grounds.

Angels, unlike haloes, appear both in pictorial form and in the written word. Both forms tend to reinforce crude anthropomorphism unless some careful teaching takes place to help the children explore their symbolic function. Regarding angels, however, it is unwise dogmatically to insist they do not exist, any more than it is wise to assert Satan did not follow Jesus of Nazareth around in a physical form (see p. 35). Instead, children can be helped to investigate the role of the angel in question, and to consider other ways in which the artist or writer could have 'got the message across' more effectively.

Angels are used in many of the world's religions to indicate that a person is receiving a divine message or gift of some kind. In essence, they can be understood as poetic, creative devices used by writers and artists to explain in vivid terms what is believed to be a religious truth or happening. Religious narratives have inspired much great art, where angels are prominent in conveying messages: for example, to Mary when she was informed she was to have a baby; and to the shepherds in the fields who were instructed to find the new-born baby in the Nazareth stable. They are depicted as giving support and comfort to the mourners at the death of Jesus of Nazareth (for example, in Giotto's painting *The Lamentation of Christ*). In Judaism, Jacob's vision was one of a ladder with angels ascending and descending, no doubt preparing the sleeper to receive God's message concerning his future prosperity. In Islam, the prophet Muhammad is believed to have received insights from Allah through the mediation of the Archangel Gabriel.

Box 5.4 provides a few examples of narratives where angels make an appearance. These could be used in conjunction with the suggested activities in Box 5.5, where ideas are given on how these 'angel appearances' could be taught to children in order to help them think beyond a literal understanding of angels as people, without necessarily dismissing it.

Box 5.4 Some examples of religious narratives featuring angels

1   Jacob was in trouble. He had cheated on his brother Esau, and Esau was preparing to kill him. Jacob had no choice but to get as far away from his brother as possible. He sped to a far-off land, and feeling weary and exhausted, lay on the ground to rest. He had only stones for pillows, but he was so tired, he was soon asleep.

Jacob had a dream, and in his dream he saw a long ladder reaching to God. Angels were moving up and down the ladder, and in his heart Jacob felt he was near God. A message seemed to come to him. God promised that he would have much land and many children. His family would spread all over the earth, and God would protect and guide him.

In the morning, Jacob used the stone he had used for a pillow to make an altar to God. He poured oil on it, and called the place Bethel. (Based on Genesis 28, vv. 10–17.)

2   Mary lived in a little house in the village of Nazareth. As she was sitting quietly one afternoon, an angel appeared to her. He told her she was special to God, and she was to have a baby, a little boy. The boy would grow up to be great, the Son of the Highest, and he was to be called Jesus. His Kingdom would never end. (Based on Luke 1, vv. 26–33.)

3   There were shepherds in a field, keeping watch over their flocks of sheep by night. Suddenly, the Angel of the Lord came to them, and glorious light shone round about them and they were afraid. The angel told them to visit the stable, where they would find a newborn baby, who would be called Christ, the Lord. The angel host began to sing:

> Glory to God in the highest,
> And on earth, peace, good will toward men.
> (Based on Luke, 2, vv. 8–14.)

4   Jesus had been killed on the cross and his body placed in a cave. His friends, weeping and terribly sad, made their way to his tomb. They were amazed to find the heavy stone had been rolled away from the cave mouth, but at least they would be able to get inside after all. They entered, but the body of Jesus was not there. They were very upset, but suddenly noticed two men,

dressed in shining robes. They bowed their faces to the ground, so bright was the light. They were told Jesus was not dead: he had risen, and they would see him again. (Based on Luke, 24, vv. 1–6.)

5 Muhammad, a young man who travelled a lot across the hot desert as part of his work, began to spend a lot of time thinking very hard. Sometimes, when the desert sun was very hot, he would seek the shade and coolness of a cave he knew, and he would lie there to rest and think.

One day, Muhammad was lying in the sandy cave when he felt he was not alone. An angel – the Angel Gabriel – stood there before him. Gabriel brought him messages from Allah. He was to learn these messages by heart and teach them to all the people he met. These messages told the people how they should treat each other and how they must obey the will, or orders, of Allah. Then all would be well.

Teaching points arising from the above narratives

There are several points arising from the above narratives which need to be addressed by teacher in order that misunderstandings can be resolved with the children. This will clear the way for the children to begin to appreciate the real theological issues which are being made. Here are two possible misunderstandings which could form in children's minds.

1 Angels are likely to be thought of in terms of human beings (as depicted throughout religious art): that is, as winged people, both adults and children. This leads young children to confuse the symbol with fairies, and is unhelpful for religious understanding.
2 Angels are likely to be confused with children's experiences of magic in stories. Again, this confusion obscures the religious points being made.

The various theological implications of angels in religious symbolism are itemised in Box 5.5, with suggestions on how teachers could help children to broaden their thinking through the medium they provide. In other words, angels can be understood as being 'vehicles' whereby theological insights are communicated.

Box 5.5 Teaching about angels: people or symbols?

- Angels are always associated with light, that is, understanding. Light is a symbol of God.

- In art, figures of angels are a means of showing which people are thinking according to God's way – i.e. those who are good, not evil.

- Angels can be thought of as messages – stimulating insight, understanding, bringing comfort.

- Angels could have been people or, more likely, personifications of people's thoughts which are inspired by God's spirit.

- Develop a theme of 'Light and Darkness' (Chapter 12) to incorporate a study of angels. Could 'light', 'angels' and 'God' mean the same thing?

- Can the children draw a picture without an angel, and without using any words, to show someone 'receiving a message' from God, i.e. developing insight? Can they think of symbols of their own?

- Discuss with the children how angels are shown when someone is struggling to understand, is in trouble, or when something important is about to happen. Can they find examples from the above narratives?

- Teach the children what is meant by metaphors like these:

  - the puppy is love (gives love)
  - the footballer is power (is powerful)
  - my birthday is happiness (makes me feel happy)
  - angels are messages (a way of showing people are in touch with God).

Example of a conversation to reinforce an understanding of symbolism

Here is an example of how a teacher could develop a pupil's comment in a way to foster an understanding of the symbolic use of angels and haloes in religion.

MARCUS: Sir, I lost my temper with my best friend yesterday – Simon.
TEACHER: Oh dear. That's a pity.

MARCUS: We had this fight, see? I cried when I got home – Simon was coming around to play but he didn't.

TEACHER: Have you seen him today, then?

MARCUS: Yes. I had a dream last night about Simon and I dreamt about what I would have to do. I would have to say I was sorry – I started the scrap. I said to him this morning 'I'm sorry, man, I shouldn't have said that yesterday.'

TEACHER: What did he say?

MARCUS: 'Oh, it's alright, man.' I feel much better now!

TEACHER: If an artist had painted you dreaming, he might have shown an angel beside your bed! What would the angel have stood for?

MARCUS: Oh, the message that I had to say sorry!

TEACHER (laughing): Yes, and if the artist painted you now he might have given you a halo to show you had done the right thing and made up!

MARCUS: I see now! Thanks!

Conclusion

It is suggested that the ideas given in this chapter could well form a major element of the content of work for the Literacy Hour required by current OFSTED legislation. The OFSTED report (1998) recommends that Religious Education should make a significant contribution to literacy teaching. To incorporate Religious Education with literacy in this way would ensure that children's innate interest in and enthusiasm for philosophic and religious thinking would find an appropriate outlet in curriculum studies.

The following chapter builds on some of the ideas presented here by examining other ways of encouraging and motivating children to think about religion through the use of signs and symbols which have proved to be stimulating for young pupils.

6

MOTIVATION AND RELIGIOUS EDUCATION

Introduction

The ways in which pupils can be motivated – that is, encouraged to learn – depend to a large extent on the interests and enthusiasm of the individual teacher, and how far he/she can relate them to the corresponding interests and enthusiasm of pupils. Nevertheless, in Religious Education especially there are several factors acknowledged to be particularly motivating for pupils if lesson content is structured around them. These are discussed in this chapter and related to what are believed to be realistic expectations of learning in the Early Years.

Personal experience

The foregoing chapters which discussed the importance of conceptual development in the growth of religious understanding had at their core the experiences of individual pupils which tend to give rise to 'ultimate questions'. They include experiences of death (either human or of pets), the mystery of suffering in the world, and the questions concerning Creation. These experiences can be described as being 'personal' in that they arise from life itself or from reflections on incidents which children undergo. They can often lead to discussion with the individual child, especially if the experience is of a personal nature – for example the death of a grandparent.

Rather different to some degree are experiences that are more collective than personal. These include images of God (usually as an old man) which feature in picture books, television advertisements, greetings cards, computer games and video tapes, together with the different levels of meaning according to which language can be interpreted and images understood. Teaching that focuses on these phenomena could arise from a chance remark of a child (for example, 'Look at this picture – it's of God in the sky') or from a 'problem' which the children are given to solve. For example, a group of six year olds was asked by a student teacher to show in their drawings that 'Abraham was a good man, trying his best to do what he thought God wanted'.

Teaching that focuses on experiences of this type is likely to be meaningful to children because the questions to be investigated arise from their own activities and thoughts. Nevertheless there are many times when teachers need to initiate new ideas, and it is on occasions such as these that careful thought needs to be given on how best to gain and retain the children's curiosity and interest.

Unknown outcomes

If analysis is made of popular fairy tales and myths – which are narratives that tend to grip pupil's imaginations – their appeal is often linked to their depiction of dangerous situations with unknown outcomes. These narratives can be remote in both historical time and geographical location – indeed, the greater the remoteness the more interest is likely to be shown! For example, a child in danger of being eaten by wild animals in the bush, in Stone Age times, is likely to engage the children's interest much more than a story of a child who helps his mother do the family shopping in the local supermarket! Why should this be, when common sense might suggest that the more familiar the events are to the child, the greater the levels of interest are likely to be?

The answer seems to relate to the conclusions children draw from experience. In the case of supermarket shopping, they seem to learn such occasions are likely to be boring and monotonous. However, the likelihood that someone could be attacked by wild animals – perhaps because this reflects their own deep worries about personal security – will cause them to listen with sustained concentration!

These points have much significance for the teacher who is attempting to select material to use with young children, particularly in Religious Education where the concepts to be developed often seem remote from the child's everyday world. In Box 6.1 are some suggested criteria which teachers might find helpful in their selection of lesson material.

Box 6.1 Criteria for selecting motivational lesson material

- Does the material relate to instinctive concerns of childhood, e.g. insecurity? (Which would be more suitable: the story of the Judaic hero, Joseph, or a story of a modern-day child playing in the garden?)
- What is there in the content of the material which is likely to futher conceptual development in religion? How will

---

teaching/responses to children's remarks deepen this? (For example, how can work on the 99 names of Allah help children understand the idea of God as many-faceted?)

- What experiences are the children likely to have undergone already which they will use to relate to this material? In other words, how are they likely to assimilate the material within the existing conceptual networks? (For example, if teaching the metaphor of God as father, what kinds of experiences of 'fathers' are they likely to have had?)

- Is the background against which the material (e.g. a story) is set new and exciting, or familiar and perhaps mundane? What are the children's reactions to it likely to be? (For example, is the material concerned with natural phenomena outside of human control, or a non-threatening subject, for example 'The Policeman Who Helps Us'?)

- In what directions will my teaching need to focus in order to ensure that the children are led forward in their understanding, rather than standing still or becoming more confused and discouraged? (For example, by telling them God is all around, without preparing material about the meaning of transcendence, i.e. non-spatial, material existence.)

- What elements in the material are new, and will the children need help in assimilating them? (For example, the teaching from Buddhism that Prince Siddhartha believed we must learn to accept what we cannot change.)

- Will the material encourage the children to think for themselves, rather than simply accepting what others say?

Jungian archetypal images

There are occasions in the life of every teacher of young children when, even if it lasts only for a second or two, for some reason one becomes aware of an intense, corporal interest throughout the classroom on some aspect of the work being taught. This often happens when a story is being read to the children and mention is made of something that immediately grips their imagination in a mysterious way. Rudolf Otto described such occasions as a conscious awareness of the 'numinous'. The intense interest felt is not dependent on experience, but rather consists of an awareness of a dimension or reality that transcends the rational: 'It may become the hushed, trembling, and speechless humility of the creature in the presence of – whom or what? In the presence of that which is a *mystery* inexpressible' (Otto, 1958, 13).

A famous passage well known for having this effect is to be found in Kenneth Grahame's *The Wind in the Willows*:

> He looked in the very eyes of the Friend and Helper, saw the backward sweep of the curved horns gleaming in the growing daylight; saw the stern hooked nose between the kindly eyes that were looking down on them . . . while the bearded mouth broke into a half-smile at the corners . . . he saw the supple hand still holding the pan-pipes only just fallen away from the parted lips; saw the splendid curves of the shaggy limbs . . . saw, last of all resting between his very hooves, sleeping soundly in entire peace and contentment, the little, round, podgy, childish form of the baby otter.
>
> (Grahame, 1983, 129–130)

Why should such a passage cause children to gain, even for a few fleeting moments, a heightened form of sensitivity? They seem to respond to the mysterious atmosphere of the growing daylight and the god holding the pan-pipes with his splendidly curved horns, sitting by the river and providing a haven for the lost otter cub.

Young children respond in a similar way to passages such as the following, based on a story from Ovid's *Metamorphoses*:

> Then a strange thing happened. The maiden felt her feet rooted to the ground so that she could no longer move them. Her outstretched arms became branches, and round her soft body grew the bark of a tree. Her hair and fingers became leaves waving in the wind – she was changed to a laurel tree!
>
> (Blyton, 1965, 29)

Transformations can take a variety of forms. While in the work of Ovid these changes are usually physical, phenomena encountered at different times in one's life can be transformed by the human psychology to fit individual concerns and experiences, often acting as standards against which to evaluate personal experience.

The philosopher Carl Jung (d. 1961) argued for the reality of what he called the 'collective unconscious', which he said comprised the experiences of humanity from the dawn of time expressed through a variety of images. Jung believed the effect of these images (which he called 'archetypes') was to recall in the corporate unconsciousness an awareness of what it was the archetype signified, resulting in moments of heightened awareness and sensitivity. He described the images that tend to excite the collective unconscious as follows:

> Here belong likewise the cellar and cave, watery depths and the

sea, as also fire, weapons and instruments . . . monsters personify primordial, cold-blooded animal nature . . . cave and sea refer to the unconscious state with its darkness and secrecy.

(Jung, 1978, 93)

As Fowler (1976, 136) stated: 'Younger children depend upon rich stories to provide images, symbols and examples for the vague but powerful impulses, feelings and aspirations forming within them.'

Tim Brighouse, Director of Education for the City of Birmingham, has said on numerous occasions that the young child ought to hear at least one thousand stories during his or her early years. The importance of this for the growth and development of values specifically, and for mental health generally, cannot be overstated, because stories and narratives rich in imagery offer children symbols against which they can evaluate their own experiences. Without their aid, the mental life of people is likely to flounder.

Personal experiences require to be united with the broader, more general insights which have become part of the collective, intuitive ability of the human race in order gradually to deepen the perception and understanding of one's personal attributes and how they interact with the immediate neighbourhood and wider society.

The power of the archetypes to grasp and retain interest was well known in the ancient world. For example, there are countless examples from the mythology of Ancient Greece and Rome of heroes diving into the depths of the sea in search of treasure, or of being set a difficult task, as was Jason in his pursuit of the Golden Fleece. The scriptures of the world religions abound in these images, and these offer teachers rich material upon which to base lessons likely to engage the interest of young children.

Box 6.2 provides examples of some archetypes drawn from Jungian psychology with suggestions of material drawn from religious writings which have the images at their heart. The suggestion is that, if the archetypes are prominent in the lesson material, what is taught has a very good chance of appealing to children.

Box 6.2 Archetypal images: a foundation for motivating interest in religion

Archetype	Suggestions for lessons
Rocks and stones	God as a 'rock'; Peter as 'the rock on which the church is built'; Jesus as a 'cornerstone'. The Kaaba Stone: its significance for the Muslim; Abraham builds the stone altar on which to sacrifice Isaac.

Light and darkness	Concepts of good and evil, right and wrong (see Chapter 12).
Water	Noah's Ark (water's cleansing properties/God's concern for the preservation of goodness); Guru Nanak's birthday (see Box A8); Jesus' baptism (see Box 10.8).
The Sword	Symbol of the fight against evil (e.g. the *kirpan* [sword] of Sikhism).
Treasure	The story of Prince Siddhartha – the four-fold nature of truth (see Box 10.4); the parables of the Prodigal Son, the Lost Coin and the Lost Sheep.
Trees	The Tree of Good and Evil (Genesis); the Buddha and the Bo tree; the crucifixion of Jesus of Nazareth.
Deserts	The revelations to Muhammad (see Box 10.6); the kidnap of Joseph by his brothers (see Box A3); the flight to Egypt of Mary and Joseph; the temptations of Jesus of Nazareth.
Fire	Moses and the Burning Bush (transcendence of God); Prince Prahlada and Holika the Witch (Hindu Festival of Holi; see Box A4).

Conclusion

The ideas provided in this chapter on ways to motivate children's interest in religious material by basing it on both personal and collective experiences (archetypal images) are developed in Part III. The next part of the book provides examples of how schools can plan the curriculum in Religious Education, both in general for the whole school and in detail for the classroom teacher.

Part III

SCHOOL PLANNING

The focus of the chapters in this third section is on school planning. It begins by discussing how the Early Years Department could plan Religious Education in such a way that some continuity could be built into the content of lessons and the themes through which they could be developed. Specific suggestions include how the Religious Education Co-ordinator could help colleagues assess the educational importance of any material they might consider teaching to their children and how the content of lessons that are familiar could be presented to pupils in new ways in order to encourage a greater depth of understanding.

The section continues by presenting detailed examples of how Religious Education could be planned and delivered to Reception, Year 1 and Year 2 classes. In many cases, the narratives around which the lessons are planned are provided in full, as they could be read to the children. Detail concerning methods of assessing and recording children's progress is also developed and, in the case of Year 2, detailed suggestions are provided of how pupils could be introduced to self-assessment.

Chapter 11 provides a discussion of Collective Worship, the controversies which surround perceptions of its role in education, pupils' reactions to the way in which worship is organised, and new insights into how Collective Worship could become part of the educational process. Attention is focused, for example, on how pupils can be expected to relate at various levels to Collective Worship, which are called the 'adoration' and 'exploration' levels.

Chapter 12 is planned primarily to assist the Religious Education Co-ordinator in the task of planning and organising Inservice Staff Development Sessions. The activities suggested are related to the text of the book, and refer also to material contained in the Appendices.

Chapter 13 the final chapter takes a broad view of Religious Education and its responsibilities in helping people – both pupils and adults – to think in an informed way about important values which are at the very core of society.

7

CURRICULUM PLANNING
A whole-school approach

Whole-school planning: why and how

For Religious Education to be educationally effective – that is, for pupils to be able to develop an interest in religion which is on-going and sustained by an ability to apply religious insights and wisdom to reflection on experience – it is essential that teachers agree on both the general aims of their teaching and also the content through which to achieve them. In other words, it is essential to have some progression built into schemes of work and this necessitates some agreement on what is to be taught and to what purpose. Of course, the detail of how this is done is the concern of individual schools, but the following guidelines should be helpful in providing a structure for long-term planning.

Identified in Box 7.1 are four targets that are basic to the teaching of religion in primary schools. Through staff consultation meetings it will be necessary for decisions to be made concerning leadership in Religious Education – it is becoming increasingly common in primary schools for a Religious Education Co-ordinator to be appointed whose role includes general leadership in the subject area and responsibility for summarising information concerning the four points in Box 7.1 for discussion by teachers.

Box 7.1 Planning the RE curriculum: four target areas

Target 1   Identifying the needs of pupils through professional observation of both individuals and the local community.

Target 2   Resources available in school – both existing materials and what additional materials might be useful.

Target 3   Appointment of an RE Co-ordinator plus the gathering of information concerning individual expertise.

Target 4   Decision-making, for example in terms of the general aims of RE and an outline of curriculum content.

The following are guidelines concerning areas of concern in Religious Education which will need to be addressed during staff consultation meetings.

Areas to be addressed concerning the planning of RE

1   Who will provide leadership in Religious Education? What form will this leadership take and what expertise is available to support him/her from (a) teaching colleagues and (b) the local community?
2   What are the aims of Religious Education to be? How will these be expressed in the school brochure? Who will have responsibility for producing a draft document for consultation?
3   What resources exist in school at present (e.g. books, film strips, slides, work-packs, religious artefacts like statues or icons, etc.)? What will need to be added to these to enable teachers to teach more effectively?
4   Regarding the focus of the curriculum, what content will be most appropriate for (a) enabling conceptual development in religion to move forward and deepen, and (b) to encourage children's developing values system to become increasingly informed by religious insight and wisdom?
5   How will time be allocated to Religious Education?
6   How can Religious Education make a contribution across the curriculum?
7   How will work in Religious Education be assessed, recorded and reported?
8   How will planning enhance the existing content of Religious Education provided by the school?
9   Plans for staff development in Religious Education (see Chapter 12 for detailed programmes of work).

School Policy Statements

Schools are required to provide a Policy Statement for Religious Education and this document is included in the school brochure. Its intention is to inform parents, and other interested parties, of the main legal stipulations concerning Religious Education and to set out the aims of Religious Education in the school curriculum with perhaps some information concerning Collective Worship and its educational purposes. The following suggestions could prove helpful for teachers who have the responsibility of preparing a draft statement for the teachers' consultative meeting, where the final Policy Statement will be agreed.

•   Keep the Policy Statement brief (an example of such a document is provided in Appendix B).

- Avoid the use of jargon – the primary purpose of the Policy Statement is to inform parents of the aims of Religious Education in the school, and their legal position under the terms of the Education Reform Act, 1988.
- Avoid statements that are vague – for example, 'to develop children's potential' – instead, provide sharp bullet points which are unlikely to be misunderstood.

Curriculum focus

It has been suggested in foregoing chapters that the greatest educational need in Religious Education is to bring about conceptual development. Past experience has shown repeatedly that it is extremely rare to find circumstances where pupils are helped to move beyond simplistic levels of an understanding of religion. As in other subjects, conceptual development in religion is not something that can be achieved in a single lesson, term's work or even school year – hopefully, schools will introduce pupils to a journey that will be life-long. Work in conceptual development should, therefore, focus on the encouragement of depth of thought, rather than the provision of set answers. To put it another way, the emphasis should be on deepening reflection by introducing new ideas and viewpoints that are stimulating and challenging and which lead to further thought.

These are the main ingredients of conceptual development in religion:

- to present narrative/story which illuminates an aspect of life (for example, the struggle between good and evil in the story of 'Cinderella') followed by discussion/activities which reinforce/encourage the pupils to question and reflect in increasingly greater depth;
- to help children become aware of depths of meaning in language through work on metaphor;
- to help children recognise and interpret religious symbolism in pictures, sculpture and architecture;
- to offer responses to pupils' questions which will encourage further reflection by introducing new material or additional examples of the point being made;
- to arrange outside visits which stimulate new visions and perspectives on life. (For example, the author well remembers how a six-year-old child asked her, during a day-trip, whether the village they were walking through was 'posh'. When asked why he thought that, he replied 'because there isn't any writing on the walls'.)
- to introduce children to music, paintings and other materials to help them move beyond the everyday – for example, by using music which enhances worship, or by providing a print of a famous painting or sculpture which is unusual. (For example, a five year old was fascinated by the picture of Ophelia floating downstream surrounded by

her garlands of flowers, as painted by the Pre-Raphaelite, John Everett Millais [1829–1896]: prints are easily obtainable in most art books.)

Box 7.2 provides an example of the type of curriculum planning which could result from a staff consultative meeting – one that respects the professional freedom of the individual teacher concerning how the material will actually be used in the classroom.

Box 7.2 Planning in RE: possible work scheme for one year

Age-groups suggested below should be thought of as being very flexible, as only teachers who know the children are in a position to assess the appropriateness of work-pitch; chronological age is not necessarily a reliable guide to potential.

The following examples show how work in Religious Education could be integrated with language development, specifically metaphor (see Chapters 3 and 4). Examples are provided in later pages of how much of the suggested content could be developed with children.

Inter-curriculum work: metaphor in language

Theme	Concepts to develop	Content	Age group
TERM ONE			
God concepts	God as creator	Creation narratives	R, 1, 2
	God as father	a good father is: – a friend; – a comforter;	R, 1, 2
		– provider of food, shelter, love, advice, guidance. (In what ways can God be thought to give us these?)	R, 1, 2
	God as a shepherd	The Good Shepherd	R
	One God, many names	99 Names of Allah: The Loving One, The Forgiver, The Kind, etc.	1, 2
	The Festival of Diwali	Rama and Sita's story; Diva Lamps; the goddess Vishnu	1
	The Festival of Hanukka	Judas Maccabeus The menorah	1, 2

	Advent	Looking forward to things Advent calendars and candles	1, 2
	Christmas	Use of lights to show Jesus came to bring new ideas and the possibility of a new lifestyle to a sad, 'dark' world	R, 1, 2

TERM TWO

Light and Darkness	God as light, darkness as distancing from God	Discuss children's experiences of darkness: when the light is switched on, how do our feelings change?	R, 1, 2
		The Temptations of Jesus	2
		The Kidnap of Joseph	R
		Palm Sunday	R
		Easter: New Life of Spring	R
		Arrest and Trial of Jesus	2
		Good Friday – Why 'Good'?	1, 2
		The Resurrection of Jesus	R, 1, 2
		Prahlada and Aunt Holika	R

TERM THREE

New Beginnings	The Significance of Change	Birthday of Guru Nanak	R
		The Prodigal Son	R
		Manifestations of Brahman	1
		Vishnu the Preserver	1
		Kali the Great Mother	1
		The Festival of Hanukka	2
		The Birthday of the Christian Church	

In addition to the above, each teacher would attempt to respond appropriately to children's questions (see Chapter 5).

Appropriate work in language which would be supported by the above ideas include introducing pupils to Greek mythology, traditional fairy tales (see Box 3.5 for ideas on how to develop 'Snow White and the Seven Dwarfs' and Box 8.1 for lesson plan on 'The Bad Wolf and the Three Little Pigs'), poems and literature that is rich in layers of possible meanings.

Selecting lesson content: criteria for assessment

The criteria for assessment that were introduced in Chapter 2 could be extremely helpful to the teacher faced with the dilemma of what to teach in Religious Education. The teacher may have in the class children from a variety of religious backgrounds and a majority of the others who have no experience of religion at all. This, combined with the extreme commercialisation and trivialising of Christmas in our society might lead the teacher to question the educational grounds for including work on the Nativity of Jesus of Nazareth in the educational curriculum. (See Chapter 12 [pp. 156–8] for suggested in-service activities on this issue; also Appendix D which gives ideas on teaching about Christmas and Easter.) Criteria which could prove useful to the RE teacher in deciding upon the value of including the Nativity story are set out below.

1 *Strict logic* Does the story make sense in that it isn't contradictory? The story does not contain contradiction but paradox. (Contradiction is like saying Gary caught the 08.15 train this morning and Gary was brought to school by his dad this morning: they cannot both be right. Paradox is like the saying 'make haste slowly', which seems contradictory but actually refers to the importance of not getting worried if you need to be quick. In a similar way 'many cooks spoil the broth' but 'many hands make light work').

2 *Consensus* Would most people agree? No, not everyone agrees with Christians, but we must help children realise that they live in a world where people do think differently. There is controversy and it is naïve to pretend there is not and to teach children to view the world in this way. It is important that they learn from the earliest age that disagreement can be civilised and that it is not the same thing as quarrelling.

3 *Explicability* Yes, it helps to explain the significance of Jesus as a real baby growing up to become a real person, whose life began in obscurity and poverty but who had remarkable insight and spiritual gifts.

4 *Workability* Not appropriate for this query.

5 *Comprehensiveness* Yes, and it relates to things meaningful to children, babies, stars, poverty and riches, as well as many more. It is, so Christians believe, about God, the Creator of the universe and all that exists.

6 *Beneficial consequences* Yes, on any showing it is one of the great stories of the world, and thinking about it can raise questions for children and for people throughout their lives: 'Is there any more to life than just the mundane and ordinary?' 'Does God exist?' 'Are Christians right or wrong about Jesus?'

7 *Relevant authority* Would most authorities agree? No, but see response to (2).

8 *Positivity* Is it like light offering a way forward? Yes, because it is uplifting and also illuminating. The thought of the importance and value of the simplest and smallest things can give all life meaning and purpose. The element of the tragic in the story reminds us that life is ambiguous and mystifying, rather than simple and therefore straightforward.

9 *Sustainability* Yes, Christians have meditated on this story for centuries and found more and more in it. People who are not Christians find it moving and thought-provoking, too.

10 *Openness* Does it encourage fresh thinking? Yes. It leads to new ideas and insights.

As the criteria indicate, the Nativity of Jesus has much to offer pupils which is of immense educational value. The teacher could well be faced with the task of helping the children perceive something fresh in the story – even by Year 2, pupils could well have become reasonably familiar with a 'straight' telling of the narrative. In Box 7.3 is given a version of the Nativity narrative which suggests to the teacher a new insight into a possible meaning, namely that the story could be showing that the teachings of Jesus of Nazareth would herald new, more responsible attitudes towards the outcasts of society.

Box 7.3 Narrative: 'The Nativity – what about the shepherds?'

Joseph had been so disappointed when the Innkeeper told him there was no room for Mary and him at the Inn. They were both so tired after their journey to Bethlehem and Mary was due to have her baby very soon. Joseph jumped at the chance of staying in the stable, which was in a cave cut in the rocky hillside at the back of the innyard.

When they had unpacked their little donkey, Joseph made a bed of straw, covered by a cloak, for Mary, and during the night she gave birth to a little baby boy. They called him Jesus. Everyone was asleep. No-one knew that a great leader of the future had been born, although his birth had been promised by prophets for hundreds of years.

But wait! Not everyone was asleep that night. The shepherds were awake. They were keeping watch over their flocks of sheep on the hillside. Very few people trusted shepherds. For one thing, they tended to be dirty, rough men with living outside so much, and for another they could never get to the synagogue services because they were always up on the hills looking after their sheep.

As the shepherds huddled together on the hillside, the cold darkness of the night seemed to grow lighter. The light became dazzling

---

and they were terribly frightened. Was it the end of the world? They seemed to hear voices singing, which told them to go to the stable in the innyard where they would find a newborn baby boy and his parents. This baby was very special: he was the one who had been promised by God long ago. He would be a great leader and teacher.

In astonishment, the shepherds stumbled down the hillside and pushed their way into the stable. Why ever should poor people like them be the first to hear the news? They looked over the planks of wood Joseph had put over the cave mouth to try to keep the wind off Mary and the baby. They started in astonishment at the young couple, lying in the dirty stable, and at the little baby lying in a cattle feeding trough, the manger. This great leader of the future was even poorer than they were!

The shepherds knelt down in amazement, feeling deeply in their hearts that this baby was very special indeed. They also could have had a feeling inside their hearts that they, and other poor people like them, might not be outcasts for ever.

The query to be tested against the criteria in order to assess this particular interpretation of the Nativity of Jesus might be:

- *Could a reasonable interpretation of the Nativity narrative be a call for greater social consciousness towards those deemed to be social outcasts? Is there any evidence this had developed since the gospel was written?*

The criteria when applied, give the following results:

1 Does it have paradoxes?	Yes. God as a baby; being born in a stable; shepherds (outcasts) being the first to hear of the birth of the long-awaited Messiah.
2 Would most people agree?	Yes, although it is something constantly debated.
3 Does it explain something?	Yes. It moves the Nativity narrative beyond a pretty story to one that challenges 'social assumptions'.
4 Is it likely to work in practice?	Yes. Improvements have been made during past centuries. In many parts of the world there is greater concern for the poor.
5 Does it cover large areas of 'experience'?	Yes – internationally and throughout all periods of time.
6 Could it be helpful?	Yes – society would be, and in many instances has, improved significantly.

7	Would most authorities agree?	Most authorities in areas where it has been implemented have seen vast improvements on past practices.
8	Does it offer a way forward?	Most definitely.
9	Does it offer support?	Most definitely.
10	Is it open to new ideas and insights?	Without a doubt.

Assessing, recording and reporting

Why assess, record and report on Religious Education?

Although, at present, there is no official requirement to assess, record or report pupils' work in Religious Education, there are a number of reasons why it might be helpful to do so. These are presented below, and could contribute to discussion at teachers' meetings.

1 It is important to record work done with children, because this allows colleagues to structure their own teaching programmes to build on and develop work already undertaken.
2 If colleagues are aware of past work, there is less chance of repetition.
3 Some record of achievement in this area makes its contribution to the all-round picture of the individual child's personality development. This could prove invaluable for providing information on material that is likely to motivate in the future.
4 Teachers' records can be a valuable source of information for future lesson planning.
5 Parents are entitled to receive information on their children's progress. Discussion of records with them can open up important dialogue and may help them see ways in which they can support their children outside of school.
6 Records in Religious Education provide an important database which can help those with an interest in the work of the school to understand the type of lessons developed with children and how it relates to the Policy Statement Document.

However, it is recommended that teachers work within several criteria when undertaking the assessment, recording and reporting of pupils' progress in Religious Education. These are discussed below.

1 *The integrity of oneself as the teacher* Can we ever be absolutely certain of the total reliability of our assessment? Dogmatic comments are to be avoided at all costs! This is very important since, especially with very

young children, their performance in any particular task is dependent on a host of circumstances, including the context in which the assessment is made, how far the child feels motivated to co-operate with the assessment procedures, and the levels of interest in the material being assessed. Many of these depend upon the wisdom of the teacher.

2   *The necessity of respectful attitudes towards both pupils and parents* What could the effects of our comments be for both.

3   *The wisdom of looking for positive ways forward*, even in the most difficult of circumstances, rather than dwelling upon present situations.

4   *The avoidance of simplistic gradings*, for example, alphabetical or numerical labelling. Although quickly recorded, there are inherent dangers lurking in their use because of their superficiality. Similar comments can be justifiably made of 'tick-lists' since these do not provide teachers with the detail necessary to make judgements concerning children's potential; nor do they make a contribution to the all-important area of development.

5   *The importance of supplying, where appropriate, evidence of children's work to support comments made*, e.g. a drawing, piece of writing, photograph or painting. Whatever theme or topic one decides to assess, it is advocated that the criteria for assessment be formulated according to the following (which will, doubtlessly, be familiar to readers):

- *Child's attitude towards others*, whether they be in the class, school, story, book or poster. For example, the writer remembers a five year old exclaiming 'Oh, poor Jacob!' on hearing how he used a stone for a pillow! On another occasion, following a reading of a version of the Creation narrative from Genesis, a six-year-old boy announced to his teacher that 'I liked the serpent the best!' Evidence such as this, if used sensitively by the teacher, can reveal a good deal about the child's developing psychology and attitudes towards others generally.

- *Child's attitude towards the environment.* Does s/he mention any aspect of a visit which afforded pleasure/enthusiasm/empathy/sorrow/humour? For example, a four-year-old child said, as she was digging in the sand during a visit to the beach, 'I'm going to ask my dad to bring me here tomorrow.'

- *Evidence of curiosity, or a wish to search for understanding.* For example, a six year old was interested in why angels and Jesus had lights above their heads in a picture-book he brought to school. His interest led to a good deal of work with the class on the theme of light and darkness.

- *Evidence of a sense of fair-play.* Instances could be recorded of times when children exclaim 'It's not fair!'

- *Appreciation of beauty* (i.e. qualities which give pleasure to the senses or mind). For example, a five year old asked if the class could sing

'Land of the Silver Birch' again because she enjoyed 'the way the different parts fit together'. In other words, she could appreciate close harmony.

Assessment

It is for the individual school to decide upon the most appropriate method of assessment for their particular needs, and this principle also applies to the type of records that are kept. There are a number of basic ways in which teachers might assess and record.

End-of-day-notes

Many teachers might feel that the best way in which they can record pupils' progress in Religious Education is to make notes at the end of the school day, perhaps including them in each pupil's file, as appropriate. These could be made quite quickly, while the lesson and associated activities are fresh in the mind. Useful headings under which such notes could be recorded include the following:

- *Pupil comment*: what it revealed about, for example, conceptual development, curiosity, general interest, or sympathy towards the material introduced during lessons.
- *Pupil statement*: a record of occasions when pupils might have made a statement which provided insights into the way in which s/he was thinking: for example, questions or assertions about the death of pets or the problem of suffering.
- *Creative/imaginative work*: notes on how far the pupil can contribute imaginative, creative ideas to the discussion, for example, by suggesting outcomes of unfinished stories or by making predictions.
- *Levels of reasoning*: the ability to reason, for example concerning Joseph's decision to forgive his brothers years after his kidnap.
- *Evidence of conceptual development*: for example, the ability to think of God in increasingly sophisticated metaphors that avoid the crudely anthropomorphic.
- *Records of any outstanding pupil responses to a particular stimulus*, for example, regarding animal welfare or natural disasters such as earthquakes.

Testing

It could be thought appropriate, in some circumstances, to test pupils' understanding, for example their development of religious concepts. However, it should always be borne in mind that, for young children especially, the *context* in which information and ideas are requested is of vital

importance for performance. Many young children will recall information, or be stimulated to reflect in depth, on circumstances or subjects
which they find exciting and meaningful. Therefore, tests which are 'out of
context' might result in performances that fail to provide information
which really does give a true indication of pupils' potential.

Recording

Box 7.4 provides a template for a pupil's record sheet for the use of teachers
who wish to record pupil's progress in tests. Of course, it is expected that
teachers would adapt this to suit their own circumstances and pupil needs.

**Box 7.4 Sample pupil record sheet: Religious Education and
values education**

Name: . . . .

Date: . . . .

Class: . . . .

Theme/topic: . . . .

Method of assessment (e.g. discussion, sample, group, individual):

Record of response by pupil to: (include here one or more of the five-
fold elements of respect: oneself, others, environment, fairness, beauty)

Teacher's comment on work sample, child's comment, etc.:

Factors found to be motivating for child:

Development plans:

(Attach, if appropriate, sample work)

Signed . . . .

The suggestion is that at least one form be filled in each half-term for each child in the class.

Pupils making assessments of lesson content

Children in Year 2 applying some criteria to lessons

Children from approximately Year 2 can be taught to use the criteria discussed earlier (pp. 92–3) in order to make an informed assessment of the ideas offered to them during lessons.

In Box 7.5 are the results of children's attempts to evaluate the Nativity of Jesus, specifically the idea presented earlier that the narrative could be suggesting a new sympathy for society's outcasts. Four children worked together on the task.

Box 7.5 Year 2 evaluating the Nativity narrative with criteria

1	Does the idea make sense?	'Yes. You would think the angels would have gone to the King, not scruffy old shepherds.'
2	Does it help us to understand?	'The story might have been saying something like "poor people matter, too".'
3	Is it likely to work?	'We don't laugh at shepherds and binmen now.'
4	Could it help?	'It might help us to be kinder to people.'

Reporting to Parents

The following suggestions are made for occasions when teachers find themselves speaking with parents about children's work:

1   Always look for something positive to say, or point out. Many parents state they feel their child could do better, but this assessment is not necessarily fair to the child.
2   Suggest ways in which the parent could help his/her child – by hearing reading at home, or perhaps by reading to the child regularly before bedtime.
3   Give parents an idea of what you are aiming to achieve in Religious Education. The vast majority of parents hope their child's behaviour and attitudes towards life in general will see some improvement as a result, and this is not an unfair longer-term aim.
4   Help parents to see the humorous side of your work.

5 Respect confidences – both of parents and their children – entrusted to you.
6 Help parents to see their child as an individual, with his/her own interests and enthusiasms, rather than encouraging comparisons to be made with siblings, either younger or older.
7 Be prepared to discuss with parents ways in which they could cope with their child's 'ultimate questions' – see Chapter 5.

8

CASE STUDY 1

Religious Education in Reception

Introduction

The ideas provided below suggest how Religious Education can introduce Reception class children to notions of right and wrong, and why it is wiser to try to bring about right, or goodness, than wrong, or evil during one's life. A particularly effective approach is to introduce the children to a variety of rich images and to help them interpret these at ever increasing depths. It must be emphasised that when teachers introduce children to new techniques of reflection in the early years, these can have a profound influence on personality development. Teaching focused in this way should be developed throughout subsequent years (and not only as a part of the individual's 'official' education) because thoughtfulness, assisted by rich imagery, will gradually become part of the personality.

Where lesson material has already been discussed in detail, page numbers are given where the material can be found. Additional material is provided too, together with examples of how teachers could attempt to develop children's ideas through both dialogue and group work.

The theme of good and bad: the importance of good

'Snow White'

Work began by the teacher letting the children watch the Disney video film of 'Snow White' (see Box 3.5 for lesson notes). For the next quarter of an hour the teacher discussed with the children which characters in 'Snow White' they really liked, of whom they felt afraid, and which characters they felt unsure of.

PAUL: I thought the witch was creepy! She might be under your bed at night!

SARAH: No, she won't be! I liked Snow White much better than I hated the witch!

TEACHER: Why was that, do you think?

MICHELLE: Because she was pretty and kind.

DAVID: She had never hurt anyone in her whole life!

MICHAEL: I liked the witch best!

TEACHER: Why was that? Didn't you feel frightened of her? I did.

MICHAEL: No! I would have liked to fight her because she was horrible. That's why I liked her – she would have given me a fight.

TEACHER: You mean the witch was exciting?

MICHAEL: Yes – but I hoped Snow White would win in the end!

CATHERINE: I liked the little animals and birds. They came to help Snow White.

TEACHER: Yes, they were kind, weren't they. So we all think Snow White and the little animals and birds were good, and the witch was bad. What about the woodcutter who took Snow White into the forest?

LISA: He was horrible like the witch.

TEACHER: But he didn't kill Snow White, did he?

PAUL: No, but he was going to, though.

KARL: The woodcutter was good, really.

TEACHER: Yes, he tried to be bad, but the good of Snow White stopped him, didn't it.

DAVID: I think the woodcutter was both good and bad.

TEACHER: Which do you think was stronger in the woodcutter, the good or bad?

CHILDREN: The good!

TEACHER: Well, I thought that tomorrow we might paint a classroom frieze of the story of Snow White in the forest. It's time for home now, but think about the story tonight so you will be ready to paint tomorrow!

The following day the teacher painted the forest on some green frieze paper and the children were given tasks as follows, working in groups:

- *Group 1*: These children drew a large girl as Snow White. The teacher had to help them with this, because they found drawing a large figure very difficult indeed. She also helped them cut it out, but the children chose which colours they wanted for Snow White's clothes. The teacher had available a few copies of the Disney book about 'Snow White' to give them some ideas.
- *Group 2*: These children were asked to draw the witch. The teacher gave them help, as she did Group 1.
- *Group 3*: The children drew and coloured in the woodcutter. Michael offered to draw the outline, as he was good at drawing, and the others helped him.
- *Group 4*: This group drew pictures of the little animals and birds which they thought might have come to the aid of Snow White.

Again, the teacher had to give them some help, especially with the size of the figures.
- *Group 5*: The children painted faces on the trunks of the trees, referring to the Disney book for ideas.

As the children worked the teacher circulated among them, giving help and reinforcing the points made previously in discussion, namely:

1   That good things – like Snow White and the animals and birds – are very important. We should try to be on the 'good' side in our own lives, like Snow White and the animals and birds.
2   That good and bad might sometimes be mixed together – like the woodcutter.
3   That Snow White is really stronger than the witch, because good is stronger than bad.

Whilst the children's artwork was drying, the teacher watched with them the next part of the video of 'Snow White', and the session closed with a discussion which reinforced the above points. The teacher told the children that, when they came into the classroom in the morning, they would see their Snow White, the witch, the woodcutter and the animals and birds all in the forest.

The teacher cut the figures out after the children had gone and when the paint had dried. She then stapled them on to the background which the children had prepared with her help. Whilst the resulting artwork might have appeared 'messy' to people unfamiliar with children's art, she pre-ferred the 'mess' because it was the children's own work. For her, of paramount importance was the discussion which the art activities had encouraged, and she planned to develop the points which she had made later.

The teacher felt satisfied that the work developed through focusing on 'Snow White' had been helpful in encouraging the children to recognise some distinctions between 'right' and 'wrong', and that 'right' is by far the most attractive alternative. In later discussions, she suggested to the chil-dren (not necessarily during set lessons but at appropriate moments throughout the school day) that it is very important for everybody that we should try to do 'good' or 'right' things. This is because 'bad' not only spoils things, but can be totally destructive.

On one occasion she took into the classroom an apple which, although rosy and attractive, she knew to be rotten inside. Her hope was that the children would be able to remember the attractive apple offered to Snow White, which proved to be deadly poisonous. She gathered the children together on the carpet area, and together they discussed how lovely the apple looked, and what it felt like to eat such a lovely sweet, shiny fruit.

She then produced a knife and cut the apple down the middle, and the children were astonished to see it was brown and rotten deep inside.

The teacher concluded the session by simply pointing out to the children that we shouldn't let 'bad' get inside us, or it would spoil us just as it was spoiling the apple. It was also suggested to the children that it is not always easy to spot what is 'good' and what is 'bad'. Therefore we have to be careful. She suggested they might like to think about this at home that evening, and perhaps tell their parents about it.

'The Bad Wolf and the Three Little Pigs'

The following day the teacher decided to reinforce the 'apple' idea by telling the children the story of 'The Bad Wolf and the Three Little Pigs'. She began by telling the children that this story was about how important it is to be very careful to chose the right things. The lesson plan she wrote is given in Box 8.1.

Box 8.1 Lesson plan for Reception: 'The Bad Wolf and the Three Little Pigs'

Subject: Religious Education
Class: Reception
Number of children: 32
Duration: 30 min.

Objectives
1   To reinforce earlier teaching which introduced the idea that it is important to 'get good things' into our lives, rather than bad.
2   To encourage the children to reflect on literature at levels beyond the superficial in order to develop values.

Materials	Story of 'The Bad Wolf and the Three Little Pigs' (see Box 8.2). Wall chart, giving pictures of the wolf and the pigs.
Introduction	Children to assemble on the carpet area. Explain that you are going to read the story of the 'Bad Wolf and the Three Little Pigs'. It is a story about how important it is to choose good, sensible things for ourselves.
Part 1	Read the story to the children, giving them every chance to join in repetitive phrases (for example, 'I'll

---

huff and I'll puff and I'll blow your house in'), to provide opportunities for emotional relief.

Part 2   Briefly discuss the story:
- Who would have liked to have lived in the house of straw?
- Who would have liked to have lived in the house of sticks?
- Who would have liked to have lived in the house of stone?
- Why?

Part 3   Children could be given a few minutes to make their own drawings of the houses, pigs and the wolf, whilst the teacher encourages them to discuss their thoughts about the story for a few minutes.

Follow-up: 'The Houses Built on Sand and on Rock' (Matt. 7, vv. 24–27; see Boxes 8.3, 8.4).

Box 8.2 Narrative: 'The Bad Wolf and the Three Little Pigs'

Once upon a time there lived a family of pigs. There was Father Pig, who spent a lot of time working deep in the forest looking for acorns, Mummy Pig and three little baby pigs. The babies were growing very fast, and they soon noticed their little house was getting far too crowded.

Mummy Pig said, 'My dear little pigs, this house is far too crowded for us. I am afraid you three youngsters will have to leave and find new houses for yourselves. Look out for the Bad Wolf though – make sure he can't catch you for his cooking-pot!'

The three little pigs said goodbye to their mother and set off. Soon they had left the forest far behind. The First Little Pig suddenly saw a man carrying heavy bundles of straw. The First Little Pig spoke to the man. He said 'Mr Man, your straw is too heavy to carry. Why don't you give some of it to me, and then you could manage to carry the straw much more easily?'

Now the First Little Pig knew he wasn't telling the truth: he didn't really mean to help the man – he just wanted to use some of his straw to build a house, but the man believed him and gave him a big pile of straw. The First Little Pig spent a long time building himself a house of straw. When it was finished, he looked at it proudly. He said to himself, 'That is a fine straw house. The Bad Wolf will never catch me now!' He went inside the straw house and shut the door.

Out of the forest came the Bad Wolf. He stopped with surprise when he saw the straw house. 'That house wasn't here this morning!' he said, and peered through the window of the straw house. He saw the first Little Pig sitting by the fire.

'Little Pig! Little Pig!' he called softly through the letterbox. 'Let me come in!'

'No! No! I can't let you in!' cried back the First Little Pig.

'Then, I'll huff, and I'll puff, and I'll huff and I'll puff and I'll blow your house in!' cried the Bad Wolf. So he huffed and he puffed, and he huffed and he puffed, and the straw house fell down! The Bad Wolf jumped on the First Little Pig and ate him all up!

Meanwhile the Second Little Pig met a man carrying sticks. He thought to himself, 'I could use those sticks to build myself a strong house!' He went up to the man and pretended he wanted to help him. He said 'Mr Man, you cannot carry all of those sticks – you will hurt your back! If you give some to me you will be helped because your load will not be so heavy.'

So the Man gave the Second Little Pig a big pile of his sticks, and the Second Little Pig built himself a stick house. 'Now', he said, when it was finished. 'The Bad Wolf will not catch me! I will be safe in my stick house.' He went inside and slammed the door shut, and bolted it as well.

Out of the forest came the Bad Wolf. He was surprised when he saw the house of sticks. 'That stick house wasn't there this morning!' he said to himself. 'I wonder who lives there?' The Bad Wolf looked in at the window and there he saw Second Little Pig washing up at his sink. He called to him softly through the letterbox.

'Little Pig! Little Pig! Let me come in!'

'Oh no, Oh no!', said the Second Little Pig. 'I can't let you in!'

'Then I'll huff and I'll puff, and I'll huff and I'll puff and I'll blow your house in!' cried the Bad Wolf. He huffed and he puffed, and he huffed and he puffed and he huffed and he puffed and the house of sticks fell in! The Bad Wolf jumped on the Second Little Pig and gobbled him up.

Meanwhile, on the other side of the forest the Third Little Pig met a man pulling a cart full of stones. 'Hello, Mr Man!' he cried. This little pig was an honest little pig, and he said to the man 'I need some stones for a house! How much money would I have to pay you for some of your stones?'

The man looked at the Third Little Pig and he said 'You are not pretending to help me, so I will give you all the stones you need. I don't want any money!' So the man gave the Third Little Pig a great big pile of stones, and the Third Little Pig built himself a lovely, strong house of stones.

Out of the forest came the Bad Wolf. When he saw the stone house he was surprised. 'That house wasn't here this morning!' he said to himself, and went to look in at the window. He saw the Third Little Pig dusting the chairs. Bad Wolf thought to himself 'That little pig looks a tasty little pig! I wonder if he'll let me in!' So he called softly through the letter box 'Little Pig! Little Pig! Let me come in!'

Third Little Pig cried, 'Oh no! Oh no! I can't let you in!'

Bad Wolf got angry. He called, 'Then I'll huff and I'll puff, and I'll huff and I'll puff and I'll blow your house in!' So he huffed and he puffed, and he huffed and he puffed, and he puffed and he huffed, and he puffed and he huffed, but he could not blow the house in! Bad Wolf got into a real temper, and he climbed on to the roof of the stone house.

But Third Little Pig was a clever little pig and he was waiting by the fireplace. Bad Wolf slid down the chimney and landed straight into the cooking-pot Third Little Pig had ready for him!

That was the end of Bad Wolf, but Third Little Pig lived safely in his stone house on the edge of the forest.

The teacher noted that the children found it important to seek and retain some type of physical contact with her whilst they listened to the story, no doubt because it provided them with a measure of security. She noticed, for example, that pupils clutched at her skirt throughout, stroked her shoes and held her free hand. She understood that allowing them to join in the repetitive phrases of the story served a similar function: one of emotional release!

After the story was finished, there were a few minutes remaining of lesson time before the children left for home. As she had planned, the teacher gave the children opportunities to talk about the story, reinforcing the idea that it is important to choose carefully and do what we can to avoid anything that will let us down.

She asked the children for their ideas on this. She was pleased when Michael suggested that when we picked fruit in the supermarket we should not choose rotten apples (he had related the story to Snow White's apple and the points made in an earlier lesson – see above). Lisa pointed out that she would never be friends 'with horrible people'. Some of the other children were mystified by this, but the teacher decided to leave them to think about it in their own time. More direct teaching on the theme would help them, in due course.

The session finished with a drawing session, when the children were invited to draw any of the characters from the story, using chalks and their blackboards, to gain more emotional release. The teacher circulated among them as they worked, encouraging them to speak about their ideas.

It was decided to tell the children the story of 'The Houses Built on Sand and on Rock' in a later lesson. The teacher did not wish to press the children to spend too long on this, but felt interested to see if they could relate this Christian parable to the story of the Three Little Pigs. The lesson plan she wrote (see Box 8.3) was detailed, as it was intended to be filed for use with later classes.

Box 8.3 Lesson plan for Reception: 'The Houses Built on Sand and on Rock'

Class: Reception
Duration: 30 min.
Subject: Religious Education

Objectives
1   To encourage the children to reflect on the importance of thinking carefully before choosing things, and to ensure we do everything possible to choose 'the best'.
2   To introduce the idea that stories teach us things that are true to life, and to encourage the children to reflect.

Materials	Story of 'The Houses Built on Sand and on Rock' (Matt. 7, vv. 24–27; see Box 8.4). Sand tray; water; rock or large stone.
Introduction	Assemble the children and tell them that this is a story about houses and people.
Part 1	Tell them the story up to the part about building the house on sand. Ask the children if they think this would be a good idea. Perhaps let a child pour water on to the sand – what happens? Then let a child pour some water on to a stone or rock – what happens now? Would it be better to build your house on sand or on rock?
Part 2	Read the remainder of the story.

Part 3	Tell the children that this story is not just about houses but also about how important it is to do things in the right way; then our lives will be more like the house built on rock than the house built on sand!
Follow-up work	Work to be linked to Science and to activities with sand tray/water; teacher circulating and reinforcing points made during the story.

Box 8.4 Narrative: 'The Houses Built on Sand and on Rock'

Once a man wanted to build a house. He wasn't sure where to build it. When he went for a walk with his wife he saw a lovely sandy beach. The man and his wife thought how lovely it would be to live in a house on the beach: they could listen to the sea, they could paddle and have such fun living on the beach. They asked some builders to build them a house, right on the sand. They thought it would be really lovely.

The builder told the man and his wife he didn't think this was a very good place to build a house, but they had made up their mind. The builders put up the house. The man and his wife were delighted. They moved in. They played in the sea, paddled and had a lovely time.

Then one night, there was a terrible storm! The man and his wife awoke to hear the waves crashing on their house! Then they saw the walls were beginning to crack open! They had to run away and ask their neighbours for shelter!

Next day they went to see the builder again. They asked him if he would build them another house. He told them that this time they should have their house built on rocks, not on the sand, because rocks are strong. That would mean their house would not fall down in a storm.

The man and his wife agreed and the builder built them a very strong house on the rocks, and this time when the storm came, the house never cracked. It stood against the wind and the waves and the man and his wife were safe inside.

Teacher's commentary: Jesus told this story. It is about houses, but it is also about how important it is to do right things: then our lives will be more like the house built on rock than the house built on sand!

The teacher told the children this story whilst they drank their milk. When it was finished, Andrew said he wouldn't have liked to have been in the house when the walls cracked open during the storm. Michelle said it was a little bit like the story of the houses the pigs built. The teacher suggested the story might be trying to teach us something very important – how we should always be careful to choose good things. Otherwise, we might pick up the poisoned apple Snow White bit into! Then we would come crashing down, just like the house built on sand had done. The children were interested in this idea, and Steven asked what the teacher meant by 'good things'. She promised to tell them another story a few days later.

Assessing, recording and reporting

On reflecting on her teaching in Religious Education, the teacher felt reasonably satisfied that the children had begun to understand a great deal. In particular, she noted in her record book that several of them had begun to realise that stories often have more than one level of meaning. For example, she recorded as follows:

- Michelle – made comments which indicate she is already able to relate ideas from one story to another, and discuss her insights.
- Andrew – enjoys detail of stories/narratives, and easily becomes emotionally involved with the content of lessons he finds engaging and exciting.

She decided that she would focus in the Literacy Hour on this very important aspect of her work with the children – helping them reflect and relate narratives (both secular and religious) to their own lives in ways that held the potential of enriching their ideas and general understanding.

At the end of each school day she noted on the children's files any occasions when she felt a statement had been made, or information volunteered, which provided evidence of how that particular child was thinking. Photographs were taken of the wall friezes made by the children, and samples of their work were included in the records.

Perhaps most importantly of all, the teacher used the children's response to the work as a guide to her future planning. In Box 8.5 is an example of the remainder of work she intended to develop in Religious Education during the last few weeks of term.

Box 8.5 Planning for RE in the second quarter of Term Two (Reception)

Week 8   The story of 'Joseph and His Brothers' (see Box A3). (This focuses on the issue of sibling rivalry, which many children may be experiencing first-hand. The subject of Joseph being forced to leave his home and family, only to be reunited later, often provides an emotional release for young children who harbour deep insecurities in this area.)

Week 9   Angels and haloes (see pp. 68–75). (Develop children's understanding of the symbol of 'light' in religious teachings: it shows understanding, happiness, God, good in the world.)

Weeks 10–12   Teaching about Christmas (see pp. 90–2 and Appendix D).

9

CASE STUDY 2

Religious Education in Year 1

Introduction

This chapter continues with the theme of how Religious Education can provide children with opportunities to learn to think in depth through a rich variety of images. Whilst the work described in the previous chapter for children in Reception classes discussed the theme of 'good and bad', the suggestion made for Year 1 pupils takes the ideas a step further by examining the images of light and darkness. 'Light and darkness' is a particularly suitable theme for this age group because all children will have undergone a variety of experiences of both. Everyone knows how daytime is characterised by light and night-time by darkness. In addition, all children will have experienced lying in bed, unable to fall asleep, and feeling afraid of the shadowy shapes dimly glimpsed in various parts of the darkened bedroom. They are equally aware of how the power of darkness quickly evaporates as soon as a light is switched on: what loomed as a terrifying monster, for example, is shown to be little more than the familiar old chair standing by the bookcase; in a similar way the frightening black 'monster' with the red eye is nothing more than the portable television set left on 'standby'.

These images are extremely rich and are fundamental to the imagery and metaphors of the world religions. It is particularly important that, from their earliest years, children are helped to unite their personal experiences of light and darkness with their role in communicating religious insight and understanding.

The following suggestions are provided as examples of how classroom work of this type can be approached. Of course, it is hoped that teachers will adapt and refine the ideas provided to do all that is possible to ensure their particular children receive material that is stimulating and motivating to their particular circumstances.

Developing the theme of light and darkness

Personal experience and light and darkness

The teacher wished to introduce the theme to the children by helping them recall their various experiences of light and darkness. He then intended to help the children transfer their ideas to a religious dimension, thereby extending their understanding of the use of the images. It is in this way that conceptual development takes place – existing ideas are used as the bedrock, or foundation, for new ideas and insights.

Box 9.1 is the lesson plan devised by the teacher for the introductory session.

Box 9.1 Lesson plan for Year 1: light and darkness in daily experience

Subject: Religious Education
Class: Year 1
Duration: 30 min.
Number of children: 33 children, aged 6.5 years

Objectives
1 To encourage the children to recall times when they had felt afraid of the dark.
2 To discuss with the children how fears caused by the dark disappear when light is introduced.
3 To reinforce the children's thoughts about the positive nature of light.

Part 1 Assemble children on carpet area. Tell them how, when I was a small boy, I lay in bed watching a strange black shadow in my bedroom. I felt so afraid that I could not even turn over in bed. I was frightened of moving my hand to the light switch in order to switch on the bedside lamp! The black shadow seemed to get more and more lifelike. I lay wondering if it could be some sort of monster – perhaps something from the time of the dinosaurs, or one of the monsters I had seen on films?

When my bedroom door suddenly opened I nearly died of shock! I felt my last hour on earth had come! Suddenly the bedroom was filled with light – my mother bent over me, and said, 'What, not asleep yet? Turn over, now, and close your eyes.'

I told her I had been imagining a monster, over there by the window. She laughed and said 'Sit up and look. The "monster" is only your bedroom chair! On it are piled your clothes for school in the morning!' She sat on my bed and stroked my hair gently, and we laughed together. 'Now, close your eyes, Philip, and sleep well. Happy dreams!'

I remember snuggling down in the warm bed and before I knew much more the sun streamed into my room and there was mother, again, pulling the curtains. 'Time to get ready for school,' she laughed, and playfully pulled the bedclothes off me. I jumped from bed at once!

Part 2   Discuss with the children occasions when they might have felt afraid of the dark. Reinforce with them how quickly our fears disappear when a light is switched on, and we can see clearly.

Part 3   Time permitting the children could write a sentence or two about their experiences of light and darkness. Both words are to be written on the blackboard, together with others that they might need.

Follow-on   According to class discussion: possibly examine other forms of light, linking work with 'bulbs and batteries' in Science. Eventually introduce religious imagery and help the children relate their existing understanding to new material.

Mr Smith found that the children listened avidly to the story he told them of one of his experiences of light and darkness when he had been about their age. He noticed with interest that several of the children with whom he had never felt particularly close seemed to warm to this weakness of his, and in general the class clamoured to share their own experiences with him. The following are some of the experiences which the children described:

- 'Once I was lying in bed. I thought somebody was trying to get in at the window. I was frightened of getting out of bed because I thought monsters under the bed would grab my feet' (Thomas).
- 'There is a road near school. The trees make it dark and spooky. We are always talking about how monsters might be there. Sometimes we think they will jump out at you' (Steven).

Katy described an occasion when she had been on holiday at the caravan:

- 'I ran outside to see my friend. It was pitch black and I was falling over. The trouble was I couldn't see anything. Then I remembered I had a little torch in my pocket so I switched it on. Then everything was alright.'

Mr Smith took the opportunity provided by Katy's comments of reminding the children what a difference light makes to darkness. Tony volunteered more information. He said he had a torch, but the battery was very low. Mr Smith said that was because the battery had run out of energy. David then said that sometimes happened to his dad's car. The battery went flat because it 'had run out of juice'. Mr Smith asked him what happened then, to be told that his dad 'charged it up'.

Mr Smith then asked the children if they could think of any times when they 'went flat', or 'ran our of energy'. Michelle told him she felt like that when she had been running fast. Laughing, Mr Smith asked her what 'charged up her battery'. There were lots of children bursting to tell him that you had a rest, or some food and drink. Mr Smith asked them if they thought this was something like moving from darkness to light. The children found this idea rather puzzling, until Robert made a comment which was really helpful. He suddenly said: 'Darkness is like when a cat is killed or when people are horrible to each other. Darkness is when someone dies in your family and everyone is sad.'

Mr Smith then asked the children if they were in a kind of darkness when they were frightened, even though it was daylight. Andrew understood the point being made. This was clear when he said 'I was in darkness when I was worrying about the spelling test.' The children laughed, and Susan added how her little sister was in darkness when she got into trouble for spilling a pint of milk.

The lesson ended by Mr Smith showing the children a picture of a lighthouse (there were a number of lighthouses near the coast, not far from the school, and the children knew about them). Andrew suddenly said, 'Lighthouses can save people's lives when they are at sea. A lighthouse guides them to shore.' Mr Smith agreed, and promised to tell the children, at another time, why people believe God is something like a light, or even a lighthouse.

The class teacher was pleased at the progress the children had made throughout the lesson. Whilst he was sure not everyone had necessarily understood all the points being made, he felt a solid foundation had been laid for later work. He respected the children's individuality, appreciating that we all respond in different ways to new ideas according to past experiences and our own ability to make links between them creatively.

Light and darkness in the Creation narrative

On reflection, Mr Smith felt pleased with the children's response to the first session on light and darkness as symbols. A couple of days later he decided to extend the work by relating the points made to explicitly religious material. He decided to introduce the children to the Creation narrative from the Jewish scriptures (Genesis 1, vv. 1–31). He decided it would be helpful to concentrate on what happened during the first 'day', and in depth on the sentence 'God said let there be light'.

He began by telling the children that many people believed that God made everything that exists. However, not everybody would agree. Some say everything is just an accident caused by science. In order to be able to work out what to believe ourselves, it is important to think a great deal about the various theories. He told them that this is what the priests who taught the Jewish people long ago wrote:

> In the beginning God created the heaven and the earth. The earth had no shape and it was empty. There was only darkness and water, but God's spirit moved over the depths. God commanded that there should be light, and light came. God saw the light and it was good. Light was separated from darkness and called Day. The darkness was called Night. And that was what happened that first day.

Mr Smith read these verses to the children once, asking them to sit very still and listen carefully. He then suggested they might like to close their eyes, even put their heads on their tables as they listened to the verses a second time. Could they think about the pictures that went through their minds as they listened to the words? These are some of the comments made by the children:

- 'It was quite spooky – cold and dark, and you wouldn't be able to see anything.'
- 'I thought there was only a tiny light moving over a storm.'
- Everything was kind of mad – no shape and dark. It was good when God made some light.'

Mr Smith asked the children if the account of Creation they had just heard was saying God might be the same thing as the light. This comment caused some argument, because whilst most of the children thought this was correct, others reckoned not, because God said 'Let there be light.' He had ordered it, so he could not *be* it! Abdulla made the perceptive point that if there is a God, we have a lot to be thankful for: it would have been horrible to have been in the darkness all the time.

Mr Smith would not let these interesting ideas pass. He took from his drawer a candle and a box of matches. He asked the children to watch as he lit the candle. As they looked at the flickering flame, he placed three nightlights which he had brought ready for Christmas on the other side of his desk, and asked the children if anyone would like to light the night-lights from the candle. Jennifer, Malcolm and Philip did so.

'Now', said Mr Smith. 'Are the nightlights the same as the candle?' The children said of course not, they were quite separate. Mr Smith went on to suggest that lots of people around the world would argue that just as the big candle could give its light away without becoming less – the light spread, in a way, to the nightlights – so many people around the world believed that God's concern for everything he made spreads. Malcolm wanted to know if that meant God was just a candle! Michael grew a little impatient with this; he responded by saying Mr Smith was trying to say lots of people believe that God works a little bit like a candle – but only in how power spreads.

This was an interesting thought. Mr Smith then told the children that the Creation account had been written long, long ago in a foreign language called Ancient Hebrew. It was possible that the people who lived then would have recited it around their campfires and that it would have helped them think about ideas of God. In that language the word for God is *ruach*, and it means energy, power, breath, the authority of God. The children did not know what 'authority' meant, so Mr Smith said anyone 'in charge' was given authority – such as Mrs Andrews, the Head Teacher. She had the job of making sure the school ran well. Could anyone think of anyone else who had authority? Kerry suggested the Queen, because she had lots of money and wore a crown. Tony said the Prime Minister, because lots of people chose him. Mr Smith reinforced the point that God's authority caused the earth to be created, and that the authority was something like light, even if it wasn't really light. He then pointed to the burning candles and asked the children to watch the flickering flames for a moment or two.

He asked the children to describe how they felt as they watched the candle burn. Tony said it made him feel calm. Lisa liked the waxy smell it made and James noticed how it flickered. He said you thought it might go out, but it didn't! All the children liked the candle flame. Mr Smith made the point that it was an example of light. He then told them how, over a hundred years ago, British soldiers who had been badly hurt in battle were lying in hospital, far away in Russia. Many of the men who were well enough to look up from their beds watched each evening for the light of a lantern to light up the darkness of their ward. They looked forward to that light because it came from the lantern of the nurse, Florence Nightingale, who gave them comfort and support when they were feeling so ill.

Mr Smith concluded the lesson by reminding the children how they had suggested in the previous lesson that lighthouses guided people away from the dangers of the rocks to the safety of the shore, or harbour. He said God was something like the lights they had been talking about. The light of God:

- helps us to see things clearly and get organised;
- gives comfort;
- gives hope.

The lesson drew to an end with the children being invited to respond to the following question. Mr Smith asked them if they could remember the story of the Three Little Pigs. The children remembered details from the story with enthusiasm. Which ones, he asked, were in darkness? Most of the children were keen to offer answers, and it was agreed that the little pigs that were eaten were in darkness. When the teacher asked why, Malcolm, for example, argued because they died. Andrea added to this the fact that they had also been stupid! Which little pig, then, could be said to have been in 'light'? Again, the children agreed unanimously that the little pig that built the house of stone was in light – to say this about him was 'another way' of saying he was safe and happy, unlike his brothers. Nevertheless, Catherine wasn't so sure. She said she thought he would have been in darkness 'a little bit' because he would be sorry about losing his two brothers.

At the end of the school day, Mr Smith noted on the children's files the various comments made by individuals and what they indicated about their levels of understanding. Box 9.2 gives an example of what he wrote.

Box 9.2 Example of teacher's notes on pupil progress in RE

Catherine Thompson. Religious Education, November 19XX

Catherine listened intently to the Creation narrative from Genesis. She was very quiet throughout the lesson, but showed she had thought deeply about the points made when she related the symbols of light and darkness to the plight of the Three Little Pigs, a story she had heard in her previous class. She argued that the third little pig was (a) in light because he had survived the wicked wolf, but (b) in darkness because he was sorry about his two brother pigs.

Date .... Class .... Signed ....

The story of the Jewish Festival of Hanukkah

Mr Smith planned to introduce his class to more explicitly religious material by studying the Jewish Festival of Hanukkah. He intended to do this by focusing on the use of the menorah, or branched candlestick which, when filled with lit candles, symbolises the thankfulness of the Jewish people for the recovery of the great Temple at Jerusalem from their Syrian enemies in 165BCE. His lesson plan is set out in Box 9.3.

Box 9.3 Lesson plan for Year 1: The Festival of Hanukkah

Subject: Religious Education
Class: Year 1
Number of children: 34
Duration: 30 min.

Objectives
1   To reinforce children's understanding of the use of light in religious symbolism.
2   To introduce them to the story of Hanukkah, particularly the use of candles to celebrate the recovery of the Temple from the enemies.

Materials   Menorah; nine candles; matches; flash cards with MENORAH written on.

Part 1   Remind the children of previous learning about light and darkness: light usually stands for either God's power or authority, or something that is characteristic of God.

Part 2   Tell the children the story of Hanukkah (see below, Box 9.4).

Part 3   Children to light the candles in the menorah from the messenger (i.e. central candle), and spend a few moments thinking about light in the world in their own way.

Mr Smith gathered the children together in the carpeted area of the classroom. He had already placed an unlit menorah on a little table, and had a box of matches ready in his pocket when the time came to light the candles. He began the lesson by telling the children he was going to tell them a very special story – something that had happened to the Jewish people over two thousand years ago, in fact – and that he would be choosing some people to light the candles of the special candlestick they could see. He produced a card, on which he had written the name MENORAH in large letters, and explained to the children this is what the special candlestick was called. They repeated its name after him. He then introduced them to the story of Judas Maccabeus and the Temple (see Box 9.4).

Box 9.4 Narrative: 'Judas Maccabeus recovers the Temple – the story of Hanukkah'

This is the story of the Jewish Festival of Hanukkah. Judas Maccabeus and his armies had been fighting for a very long time against their enemies, the Syrians. The Jews, led by Judas, had been horrified to hear stories about what the Syrians had done to their Temple in Jerusalem since they had taken over the city. Now that Judas had led the Jewish people to victory, they were on their way to Jerusalem to make it a Jewish city again.

Reports had come to the Jews that their Temple had been made into a marketplace. All kinds of food and vegetables, pots and pans and animals were for sale in some of the most holy places of the Jews. Even pork – a meat which Jews never eat – had been on sale there. Sacrifices had been made by the Jews' enemies at the very altar where they had worshipped Yahew, their own God. The Syrians had even put up a huge statue of one of their gods, Zeus. The beautiful Temple furniture had been broken and the tiles of the floors smashed to pieces.

What a terrible sight met the eyes of the Jews as they entered the Temple again! What a huge amount of work had to be done! The weeds growing from the Temple floor were dug up and new tiles were laid; the cupboards were washed and filled with new candles, cups and glass vases. Clean, new curtains were hung in the Temple and all signs of the Syrians were washed away.

Judas Maccabeus ordered his soldiers to repair the city wall of Jerusalem in case the Syrians attacked again. He then gave orders that there was to be an eight-day festival – the Festival of Lights – to give thanks to the Lord for their great victory.

Even since that time long ago the menorah, or eight-branched candlestick, has been used in the Jewish Festival of Hanukkah. The central candle is lit first – it is called the messenger – and each of the other candles is lit from it. By doing this, the Jews celebrated that light had come back into their world: the Temple, the house of the Lord, had been made clean. At Hanukkah, the candles blaze out the message of God's presence among his people.

At the end of the story, Mr Smith solemnly lit the messenger of the menorah, whilst the children watched. He then lit a taper from it, and children took turns at carefully lighting each of the candles. Soon the classroom was ablaze with light. Mr Smith pointed out what a good thing it is to share light: even though the messenger had lit all the other eight candles, its own light was just as bright as it had been at the beginning!

He went on to suggest to the children that light can also remind us of God's love shining throughout the created universe. At this point David reminded everybody that God had made the first light, before anything else existed – apart from water and darkness. Mr Smith then further suggested it might be worthwhile thinking for a moment how important it was that everyone tried to keep light burning in their own lives.

The classroom lights were switched off. The session closed by giving the children two minutes in which to watch the burning candles of the menorah. Mr Smith invited them to think about light in their own way. It might be the light of the Creation, the light of the menorah and what it meant to those Jews who cleaned their Temple so long ago, or it could be light in our own lives.

Recording, assessment and reporting

Mr Smith felt happy with the work done by the children. It was shown in Box 9.2 how he recorded significant responses on individual children's record sheets. In addition, he recorded the work done with the class for his own records, considering it would be a valuable resource for future classes, but also because it was important to create records that would be useful in future work schemes and lesson planning for the following half term. In Box 9.5, Mr Smith's records are reproduced as an example of record-keeping in Religious Education.

Box 9.5 Record of work done with Year 1, autumn term

1 *Introductory activities: children's experiences of light and darkness.* They were encouraged to recount their experiences of both symbols after the teacher told them about an incident from his own childhood which could be symbolised by light and darkness. In discussion, the children offered their own ideas.

2 *Work developed on the Creation narrative from Genesis Chapter 1.* Concentrated on God's authority as light. Children needed a good deal of help on this. Relating light and darkness to the well-loved story of the Three Little Pigs was found to be very helpful.

---

3 *Introduction to the story of the Festival of Hanukkah.* The menorah was lit, and time given to reflection about any aspect of light studied, or about light in their own lives.

4 *Follow-up/development.* I intend developing this theme during the run-up to Christmas by work on angels, haloes and all types of light, emphasising how candles and all colourful decorations point towards the presence of God. Particularly for teaching about Advent, I shall teach the children about the Advent Candle – how it stands for the coming of Jesus (the candle flame) into an otherwise sad, dark world.

10

CASE STUDY 3

Religious Education in Year 2

Introduction

Samples of work given in previous chapters focused on developing children's concepts of God by encouraging them to diversify the metaphors commonly used to express religious insight and ideas. For young children especially the symbols of light and darkness are of particular significance because everyone has direct, personal experience of both. Therefore work in Religious Education can be planned which helps pupils deepen their thinking about religion by explaining why 'good' is symbolised by light and 'bad' by darkness. Gradually, conceptual development can be furthered by considering the phenomenon of shadows and where one should move at times of crisis. What do religions offer by way of wisdom which can help us make an informed, wise decision at such times?

Developing classroom work

The theme of light and darkness

The work for Year 2 children described in this chapter was planned as a development of earlier lessons based on this theme. The teacher, Mrs Alexander, had noticed how a number of her pupils had expressed an interest in times when one is faced with making a choice. On a trivial level, Simon had told her how he had been given the choice of a birthday present from his parents: either a portable television set for his bedroom or a new bicycle. He had told her that it had been very difficult to make up his mind because he wanted both! However, his mother and father told him in no uncertain terms that he could have only one of the two things. At last he decided on a bicycle, because he could share it with his friends. He was of the opinion that nobody would have been very interested in watching his television with him.

Another pupil, however, had been faced with making a much more serious choice, and one that continued to haunt the children involved for years afterwards. Mrs Alexander was told by Elizabeth, another of her pupils, about a time when she had faced the necessity of choosing. Her parents had a major argument one Christmas Eve and told their two children, Elizabeth and her younger sister Emma, that they would have to choose whom to live with from then onwards because they were 'splitting up'. Elizabeth said they both had cried. Emma chose to stay with her father whilst she decided to leave with her mother. The latter had packed a suitcase and left the little family home at midnight. However, the night was cold and the mother had nowhere to go. She walked the streets with Elizabeth for about an hour and had no alternative but to return home and make peace with the father. Elizabeth said she had never forgotten that night, and whilst her parents had stayed together since, she and Emma never felt certain that trouble wouldn't blow up at any time and that they might be requested to make that terrible choice again.

Experiences of this type provided a basis from which much important work in Religious Education can be developed. This is because they illuminate for people the need to think very carefully about life's priorities and the necessity of making choices. Decisions made can have far-reaching results.

After discussing with the children times when they had made an important decision or choice, Mrs Alexander planned and taught the following series of lessons (see Boxes 10.1, 10.2) with the overall intention of giving the children yardsticks which could prove helpful not only in the near future but for years to come.

Box 10.1 Lesson plan for Year 2: 'King Midas Learns about Treasure'

Subject: Religious Education
Class: Year 2
No. of children: 32
Duration: 30–35 min.

Objectives
1   To help the children reflect on how important it is to recognise the really important things in life.
2   To illumine the significance of making choices.

Materials   Story of 'Midas and the Golden Touch' (see below, Box 10.2); writing materials; crayons.

Introduction Tell the children that the story I will read them was written many hundreds of years ago, in Ancient Greece. As they listen to it, will they work out an answer to this question: 'What message does the story have for us today?'

Part 1	Read the story.
Part 2	Discuss the story with the children, asking for their comments. Emphasise the difference between the things the King valued at the beginning of the story and how his choices had changed by the end. Why was this?
Part 3	Discuss with the children how the story can be true for us today. What kind of things are really important to us? Why is this? Is the story true, even though it couldn't have really happened?
Part 4	The children will be asked to think about things that are really important to them. They will then be asked to write about them in a few sentences and perhaps do drawings.
Follow-on	Further work to be developed on levels of meaning in narratives, and the importance of making wise choices and decisions.

Box 10.2 Narrative: 'King Midas and the Golden Touch'

King Midas loved gold. He collected all the gold he could find and he loved to feel it run through his fingers. He loved its dull, golden colour and looked forward to each afternoon when he could sit in his office, away from his family, counting how many gold coins he had in his treasure chest.

One day the god Bacchus decided to pay Midas a visit. The King had once done a favour for the god and in return Bacchus told him he could make a wish and it would be granted. Midas didn't need to think for very long: straight away he told the god he would like everything he touched to turn into gold. Bacchus looked very worried.

'Are you certain that is what you want?' he asked. 'Are you absolutely certain?'

'Yes, yes,' said the King with impatience. 'Grant me the wish quickly! Let everything that I touch turn into gold!' Sadly, the god left him, telling him his wish would be granted as soon as he rose from his bed the following morning.

Midas could hardly sleep for excitement. As soon as the sun's rays shone through his curtains, he leapt from bed. He noticed that the sheets on his bed had turned to gold because he had touched them with his fingers. In excitement he made his way to the palace dining room.

The breakfast table was covered with delicious food. The King was hungry. Eagerly he piled his plate with grapes, bread, eggs and many other foods. However, a strange, cold fear clutched his heart as he found the grapes turned to gold as soon as they touched his lips! The same happened to everything he touched. Midas began to panic. Would he ever be able to eat again? Was he going to starve?

In despair, the King went outside into the palace gardens. Even the roses and daisies that he touched turned to gold, stiffening on their stems and losing their perfume and colour. Midas sat on a seat in the garden and put his head into his hands. Whatever should he do?

Suddenly his little daughter saw her father, and she came running up behind him playfully. How many times had the King sent her away when she had interrupted his money-counting! She threw her arms around him from behind, laughing. In terror, the King cried out to warn her not to touch him – but it was too late! When he turned, the little girl had changed into a stiff, cold golden statue!

Rushing into the palace, the King sent a messenger to the god Bacchus, asking him to come to him at once. The god came instantly. 'Well', he said, 'did you not get our gift of the golden touch? Are you happy yet?'

The King threw himself on his knees and clutched the god's robe. 'Please forgive my greed! Take this curse from me!' he cried. 'I have learnt a terrible lesson today!'

'Go to the river which flows through the palace grounds', ordered Bacchus. 'Swim in its waters and the curse will leave you. You have learnt something of the greatest importance today, and you must never forget it.'

King Midas did as the god commanded. He noticed, when he came out of the water, that everything he had turned to gold now returned to its normal self. He couldn't get to the little golden statue quickly enough! He splashed it with water from the little stream and kissed the little golden cheeks and held the statue close to his heart. He felt it move! His daughter was returning to life!

'Father,' said the princess. 'I have just had the strangest dream! I felt so odd!' The King drew her even closer to him, and stroked her beautiful hair.

'My child', he said, 'it is I who have been dreaming, but now I am awake! My dream has lasted for years, but now I am free from its spell!' The princess looked at her father in astonishment and ran laughing to play among the flowers and trees in the garden.

> That very day the King gave his gold to the beggars at the palace gates. He felt a very happy man. His new-found happiness was worth more than all the gold in the world!

Mrs Alexander discussed the ideas raised in the story with the children. They all agreed that at the beginning of the story the King had been really foolish but that, by its end, he had learnt a very important lesson. Mrs Alexander asked them if they thought the story was true, and some mixed answers were offered. For example, Alan felt the story wasn't true, because nobody could ever have turned things into gold. Lisa agreed with him, but added that wanting more and more gold was a little like wanting more and more money so you could buy things in the shops.

Stuart mentioned that he'd noticed how quickly you get tired of your Christmas presents. He said when he had received a keyboard he had been thrilled, but now it just lay under his bed and he never touched it. Most of the children agreed with this. Kelly remarked how her mother occasionally tidied her bedroom and put the toys she never played with into sacks and they were sold at the next car boot sale. She said she loved getting lots of presents but usually only played with a few. You soon got tired of them.

Mrs Alexander suggested to the children the story could be true in a special way. Could anyone think what it might be? After a few suggestions, Paul said it make him think of times when he had been away from home, staying with his grandmother, and he had begun to worry about his parents. It was on such occasions, he admitted, that he began to realise that his parents were the most important things in his life. Mrs Alexander suggested that this was, perhaps, what King Midas's story was about: he had to do something foolish to learn how much he loved other things, such as his daughter. In that way, the story was true.

When she asked the children if they thought King Midas was in darkness or light, there was a mixed reaction. Some of the children argued he was in darkness because he was silly and his silliness made him unhappy, but the majority felt he had been in darkness at the beginning of the story but in light by the end. Mrs Alexander noted none of the children thought of 'light and darkness' in this context as physical phenomena; they had all understood the symbolic use of the terms.

The children then wrote about what they considered to be their 'treasures'. They all felt sure Midas would have written about his daughter. These are some of the things they wrote:

- 'My treasure is my cat, Tibby. I love her and we play together. Money could not buy her from me' (Andrew).

- 'After my dog died I felt really sad and I cried. My dad gave me her collar and lead. I keep them by my bed because they remind me of her and I will keep them forever' (Elizabeth).
- 'My greatest treasure is a photograph I have of my mother, before she had the illness that made her blind. That is my best treasure' (Sarah).

Mrs Alexander felt quite pleased at the end of the lesson that the children had learnt at least two important things about life: first, that we need to make choices very carefully indeed so that we recognise what is really important and, second, that stories might not have happened in history but, nevertheless, they are true in other ways.

Prince Siddhartha (the Buddha) makes an important decision

Mrs Alexander now planned a lesson which would offer the children more food for thought, and found a comment from one child particularly helpful. Peter confided in her one morning that he was very worried because he had heard his mother and father discussing the possibility of the factory where his dad worked closing down before Christmas. Peter said he was worried because his parents were wondering if they would have enough money to pay the gas bill if his father lost his job.

Mrs Alexander suggested to Peter that he should try not to worry too much as he couldn't really do anything about it. Indeed, if his parents thought he was worried it would make things even more difficult, because then they would have him to worry about too! She also pointed out that it was not certain that the factory would close, after all. Why get worried about something we cannot control and which might never happen? Peter agreed with her, and went off feeling much happier. Mrs Alexander decided, largely as a result of this conversation, to introduce the children to the story of Prince Siddhartha. The lesson she planned is set out in Box 10.3.

Box 10.3 Lesson plan for Year 2: 'Prince Siddhartha's Search for Truth'

Subject: Religious Education
Class: Year 2
No. pupils: 33
Duration: 30 min.

Objectives
1   To introduce the idea that we cannot hide away from what is true.
2   To teach the insight that thinking about experience is very important in helping us understand things that happen to us.

Materials	Statue of the Buddha, or a picture. Story of Prince Siddhartha (see Box 10.4).
Introduction	Show the children the statue (or picture) of the Buddha, and explain it is of a man who was born a Prince many years ago, in India. He was called Prince Siddhartha, which means 'A Wish Come True'. Today we are going to hear his story and discover what we can learn from it.
Part 1	Read the story of Prince Siddhartha's childhood, and his decision to explore the world outside the palace gates.
Part 2	Discuss with the children their reactions to the story: • Was he wise or foolish to disobey his father? • Was his father wise or foolish to try to keep him in the palace and its gardens only? • Was Prince Siddhartha wise or foolish to leave the palace and give up his title of 'Prince'?
Part 3	Discuss with the children the Prince's decision to throw away all his costly, valuable clothes and to abandon life in the palace. Can they think of ways in which he is a bit like King Midas? Do the children think Siddhartha was wise or foolish? Tell them that many people throughout the world try to follow his teachings and call themselves Buddhists. One of the things they believe is that it is foolish to worry about things that we cannot change.
Part 4	Children to study the picture/statue of the Buddha for a few moments, thinking about his life in the palace and its gardens. Why do they think he was not satisfied with the life of luxury? Is this something like when we grow tired of our presents (as discussed in previous lesson)? What does this tell us about humans?

The version of Prince Siddhartha's story which Mrs Alexander used is given in Box 10.4. (Note: the second part of the story is given in Box A2 in Appendix E.)

Box 10.4 Narrative: 'Prince Siddhartha (the Buddha) Searches for Truth'

About two and a half thousand years ago a Prince was born in India. His parents called him Siddhartha, which means 'A Wish Come True'. His father, the King, wanted his little son to grow up to be a powerful King, and worried that this might not happen.

He called together all his wise men and asked them to foretell what kind of life his precious little son would have. Some said he would become an Emperor, whilst others said he would become a very poor monk and teacher. The last wise man said he would become a monk who was different from all others. He would learn to understand the real truth about life. This would begin when he saw four things: an old person, a sick person, a dead person and a monk. What he saw would cause him to leave his home in the palace and begin afresh.

This made the King more worried than ever. He wanted his son to take over from him after he died. What would happen to the kingdom without a King? He gave orders that his son must never see the nasty things of life, such as death, illness and old age. To make sure of this, his little boy was never to be allowed outside of the palace gates and he was to be showered with the most expensive gifts the royal family could afford.

As the Prince grew up, he was not allowed to see any dead things: even dead flowers in the palace gardens were picked before he saw them and death was never mentioned. Three palaces were built for him, lots of people visited and he always got whatever he wanted. He married a beautiful girl and it seemed that everything his father had planned was going to happen – he would never see death, illness or old age. He was happily married and had a son. His father was certain his son would not wish to leave his wonderful home and happy life.

However, the Prince began to feel bored with his luxurious life at home. He wanted to see what was beyond the palace walls. He ordered his chariot driver to take him into the outside world. Into the street the chariot was driven. The first sight he saw was an old, bent man whose legs were covered with sores. His skin was wrinkled and his hair thin and grey. The Prince was horrified and felt sorry for the man. He asked his chariot driver what was wrong with him. He was filled with fear to learn that everybody grows old, if they live long enough, and that he himself would be like that one day, if he did not die early.

On another visit outside of the palace the prince saw a man with sores and boils, whose face was lined with pain. Whenever he tried to hobble up the street he cried out because of the disease which had attacked his bones. The Prince was shocked to learn that anyone can catch a disease, including himself, even though he was a prince.

On yet another occasion when he visited the land outside of the palace, Siddhartha saw a group of people crying as they carried someone who was wrapped in a cloth. The Prince was told that the man had died and his friends were crying because they would never see him again. Even a prince must die one day, he was told – there was no escape from death. Siddhartha could hardly believe it! He realised he hardly knew anything about life!

His life of plenty at the palace meant nothing to him now. The Prince knew that he must go away, alone, to search for the truth about life. To live here in the palace was a waste of his precious time, and he knew he must search for peace, both for himself and so he could help others. One night, when everyone lay sleeping, the Prince left his home, taking with him his chariot driver. When they were a distance from the palace he took off his costly robes, cut off his beautiful hair and gave both to the driver. He told him to give these things to his father, the King. He was to tell him not to worry: his son was safe and he was happy because now for the first time he was free!

Siddhartha had taken the first step on his search for Truth. He became a monk, just as the wise man had predicted years before. One of the things he learnt to believe was this: we are foolish to worry about things that we can never change.

Today there are many people throughout the world called Buddhists who share in this search. The last wise man's predictions had come true!

Mrs Alexander observed her pupils carefully throughout the reading of the story. When she asked them whether they thought the Prince was wise or foolish to leave his wonderful home and life in the palace the children were eager to contribute their ideas to discussion. Katy felt the Prince had definitely done the right thing, because he had been really bored. She said she knew what it was like to feel like that, when 'you are tired with all the things, like your birthday presents, which you thought you would never get sick of.' Stuart agreed, adding that the King should have let his son do as he wanted. Michael said he couldn't wait until he had grown up, because 'Then you can do more or less what you want to do: grown-ups cannot stop you.' All of the children agreed with this!

Mrs Alexander then asked the children what they thought about the Prince's belief that we shouldn't worry too much about things that we cannot change. They agreed this was very difficult indeed. Alison mentioned how she worried about her grandmother who was in hospital, even though she could not do anything to help. Susan retorted immediately that she could do something: if she did not worry, her grandmother would be less worried about *her*, and therefore would feel better. Mrs Alexander agreed with this, and felt pleased. The children were beginning to think in depth for themselves.

Before leaving the classroom that evening, she made the following notes in her record book about the development of the children's work in Religious Education. These are the important points which she identified, and which she planned to develop throughout her teaching.

1   The children were able to apply the wisdom contained in religious narratives to their own experiences.
2   They could think philosophically – that is, they could use experiences as a basis from which to make predictions of cause and effects in human life, and would attempt to understand the significance of both decisions made and the importance for the future.
3   The children could understand the idea that sometimes we reach a type of 'crossroads' in our life, when priorities selected have considerable influence on the future.
4   The children's comments demonstrated the importance they gave to 'fairness', in particular the unfairness of the King in trying to plan out his son's life, rather than giving him the freedom to which they felt he was entitled.
5   The children had been absorbed by Siddhartha's story. This seemed to be because of the mystery confronted by the Prince, namely what lay beyond the palace gardens. The historical truth of the story did not seem important. Rather, they were interested in the philosophical points made, and this was because they were both grounded within their own experiences and yet had the depth to extend their thinking concerning them.

The visions of Muhammad

A few days later one of the children in the class asked Mrs Alexander if she could tell him something. Naturally she gave him every encouragement, and the child told her he had been playing hide and seek in the garden the previous evening. His brothers ran off to hide and his sister was 'catcher'. He said he ran to the long grass in the corner of the field and lay down, flat. His heart had been pounding and he felt sure Natasha, his sister, would be able to hear it.

However, the minutes ticked over and no-one found his hiding place. Paul said he began to enjoy being alone. He liked the smell of the grass. It had a damp, funny smell, like an old church he had visited with his grand-father. He also liked looking at the stems of the grass around him, and noticed a little ladybird climbing up a stem. He began to count the colours he could see, and reached twelve when suddenly someone pounced on him. It was Robert, his brother, who had come to tell him it was time to go in the house for supper. Paul told Mrs Alexander he had really enjoyed the quietness. She suggested to him that what he had felt was being very close to nature. Paul agreed, and went off to get on with his work.

Mrs Alexander bore this interesting account in mind when she was plan-ning her next lesson in Religious Education especially, but also intended to use ideas from it in English. She could understand how it could form the core of studies in literacy. Box 10.5 sets out the lesson plan which she wrote, where she linked up a human experience perhaps similar to that of Paul which changed much of the society of the Middle East.

Box 10.5 Lesson plan for Year 2: 'Muhammad's Vision'

Subjects: Religious Education and Literacy Hour
Class: Year 2
No. children: 28
Duration: 30 min.

Objectives
1   To teach the children about Muhammad's vision in the cave.
2   To encourage the children to talk abut times when they enjoyed a time of silence and had a chance to think for themselves.
3   To teach the children the use of angels and light in religious symbolism.
4   To develop conceptual work on the symbols of light and darkness.

Materials   Pictures of angels; candles.

Part 1   Show children the pictures of angels – one poster avail-able and a number of postcards. Ask them what they think about them.

Part 2   Tell/read the children the story of Muhammad's vision (Box 10.6).

Part 3   Discuss the story with the children. What thoughts do they have about the Archangel Gabriel? Was he a person or could it be the way in which we use picture language to show someone was in close touch with God?

Part 4   Children to fill in, using their own words, the part of the
story which is missing. The following is the worksheet
they will be given:

'Muhammad in the Cave'

Can you fill in the missing part of the story below? Here are some
words to help you:

desert   cave   Archangel Gabriel   dream   Allah   visions   asleep
lying   sand   mid-day sun   tired

* * *

It was a very hot day. Muhammad had been travelling, but made up
his mind to shelter from the heat of the mid-day sun by lying in a
cool, desert cave.

. . . .

. . . .

. . . .

. . . .

Muhammad said he met the angel many times. He wrote down all
the messages he heard. They were later collected together. The book
where they can be found is called the Qur'ān. It is the holy book of
Islam, one of the great world religions.

Box 10.6 Narrative: 'Muhammad's Vision in the Desert Cave'

Muhammad, a young man who travelled across the desert in Arabia
as part of his work, began to spend much of his time deep in thought.
He was really interested in religion and sometimes when the sun
was high in the desert sky and everywhere was almost unbearably
hot, he would go into a cool cave and lie there alone, thinking. He
was worried about his people because the gods whom they worshipped did not seem to help them lead good, happy lives.

When he was about forty, Muhammad had a vision so powerful that
it was to change his life, and that of millions of people in the future. His
ideas would lead to the great world religion of Islam. Lying alone in the
cool, sandy cave, he seemed to see the Archangel Gabriel standing

before him. The angel was a messenger from God, whom Muhammad called Allah. Gabriel spoke with Muhammad and commanded him to learn by heart the messages which he had brought from Allah.

Muhammad went home and told his wife what had happened. At other times when he visited the cave to rest he again received visits from Gabriel, and more messages were given. Muhammad and his friends learnt the messages off by heart and taught them to the people who joined them.

The faith known as Islam had started, and its followers became known as Muslims. As time went on, more and more people began to believe Muhammad was the prophet of Allah, and tried to follow his example.

Muhammad always argued that an angel really did appear to him. He said he had not been dreaming. Whatever did happen changed the world, and the messages Muhammad received were written down. The book is called the Qur'ān, and it is the holy book of Islam.

Whilst the children worked at their task, Mrs Alexander circulated among them, talking with them and discussing their ideas. She was particularly interested to hear their thoughts about the Archangel Gabriel. Here is a conversation she had with a group of children.

TEACHER What do you think happened to Muhammad? Do you think he saw an angel, or what?

DAVID I don't believe in angels. They might have lived then, but not now, though.

LUCY I saw a picture of an angel on Mrs Alexander's cards. They must have been alive.

TEACHER Let's have another look at the angel pictures. [*Produces the cards.*] What can you see there?

PAUL They have got great big wings and light around their heads, a bit like Jesus.

LISA The light might mean they are on the side of good!

TEACHER Yes, excellent, Lisa. That's exactly right! What about the wings, though? What else has wings?

KELLY Birds and aeroplanes.

TEACHER What do things which have wings actually do?

PAUL They move about! Angels must move about, then!

TEACHER Yes, that's about right. If we go off in an aeroplane we might be going on holiday! Do you think that is why Gabriel visited Muhammad?

LISA [*laughing*] No! No! He flew down to see Muhammad to give him messages. He wasn't on holiday, though!

TEACHER Muhammad always said the angel really did come. Some people believe angels in stories and pictures is a nice way of showing God is in close touch with someone.

PAUL Like Gabriel was a messenger from Allah?

TEACHER That's right. So it's not really important whether the angel really exists or not.

DAVID Yes. What matters is that Muhammad got messages from God.

TEACHER Exactly. The light around Gabriel is to show he is definitely taking good messages to Muhammad.

KELLY It doesn't really matter whether there are angels or not, does it?

PAUL That is what we just said! Angels, light, God, they are really the same thing, aren't they?

TEACHER Yes. We have to make up our own minds about whether angels ever lived. I agree with Paul. We will talk more about angels another time.

Afterwards, Mrs Alexander decided to extend the children's work by focusing on the baptism of Jesus of Nazareth. In particular, she wished to reinforce what the children had already learnt about the use of symbolism in religion, both pictures and the written word.

The baptism of Jesus of Nazareth

A few days after the above lesson, David told Mrs Alexander that he was going to a christening. She asked him what he understood by this, and was informed that his baby cousin was 'to get his name'. Mrs Alexander said Jesus of Nazareth had been 'christened' too, but people usually call it 'baptism'. She wrote this word on a card, in large letters, and pinned it up beside the carpet area. Gathering the children together, she told them about the baptism of Jesus of Nazareth (Boxes 10.7–10.8).

Box 10.7 Lesson plan for Year 2: 'The Baptism of Jesus of Nazareth'

Subject: Religious Education
Class: Year 2
No. children: 29
Duration: 15 min.

Objectives
1 To extend the children's understanding of symbolism in language.
2 To introduce the symbolism of water in baptism.

Materials   Soap, bowl of water, towel. If possible, an illustration of the Baptism of Jesus of Nazareth – many are available in Christian literature and children's Bibles. Crayons, drawing paper.

Part 1   Ask the children if they have ever been to a christening ceremony. Give them encouragement to describe what they experienced. Emphasise the use of water – in the case of Jesus' baptism, the River Jordan.

Part 2   Discuss the uses of water as a cleansing agent with the children: have they experienced being called into the house to have a bath, have their hair washed, to wash their hands before a meal? Why (because germs grow on dirt and can make us ill)? To reinforce this, a child with dirty hands could wash them in the bowl, and the others observe the difference a wash makes!

Part 3   Tell the children the story of Jesus' baptism, if possible showing the children an illustration.

Part 4   Why do the children think Jesus was 'washed' in the River Jordan? It wasn't because he needed a bath: his skin was clean! We cannot wash our insides! All we can do is show something important has happened: when someone is baptised a promise is made they will do everything possible to do only good things whilst they live. In this way they are 'clean' inside, like our bodies are clean after being washed! That is why water is used for baptisms (christenings).

Part 5   Suggest to the children that the dove, and the mention of God's 'voice' could be the way the writer tells us Jesus' baptism worked really well.

Part 6   Time permitting the children could draw either (a) pictures of any baptisms they could have attended, or (b) Jesus' baptism. These drawings will be used in later discussion.

Box 10.8 Narrative: 'The Baptism of Jesus of Nazareth'

Jesus had just made a very important choice. He had decided he would give his whole life to God, teaching the people and trying to help them understand how to live their lives in order to be really happy and contented.

As Jesus was travelling along the road by the side of the River Jordan, he saw lots of people in the distance, by the river bank. He went closer to see what was happening. People were walking into the river, bending down under the water and there was his cousin, John, giving them a special blessing! He told the people to be prepared: they had made a fresh start by washing in the river. They ought to be ready to begin a new life, because someone of great importance was about to come to them.

Jesus went nearer, and his cousin saw him. He called 'This man who is coming is much greater than me! I am not important enough to bend down and untie his sandals!'

Going up to John, Jesus asked him to baptise him. John told him he ought to be baptising him, John, not the other way around! Jesus insisted, and made his way into the River Jordan. He bent down under the water, as the others had done, and his cousin gave him the blessing.

As soon as Jesus had been baptised, he came up from the water. Heaven seemed to open for him and he saw the spirit of God, coming down like a dove, and resting on him. A voice said from heaven 'This is my own dear Son, with whom I am well pleased.'

Mrs Alexander gave her pupils a few minutes to discuss the story. David said it was like the christening ceremony he would be going to in a few day's time. However, Mrs Alexander said christening wasn't just about a baby 'getting his or her name'. It was much more important. The thing to think about was water. She asked the children why they thought the people might have been bending down in the water.

Paul said he had been a little frightened they would drown, especially Jesus. Mrs Alexander pointed out water does other things than drown people! What else is it useful for? Michelle pointed out we need it to cook with, whilst Simon said you could get washed in it. This was the cue Mrs Alexander had been wanting: she went on to make the following points about water, especially water at baptisms.

- Water cleans both ourselves, and anything that has become dirty.
- Water refreshes us – we feel more lively after washing our face, or having a bath.

- People usually wash themselves before some important event, such as a party, or a holiday, because it is good to make a new start and to feel good.

She went on to ask the children if any of these things could have been important for Jesus' baptism. David said he thought it was very important because it said at the start of the story that he had just made up his mind to teach people, and help them understand more about God. Mrs Alexander agreed. She went on to tell the children that this was the purpose of baptism. The baby cousin of David would become a Christian on Sunday when he received his name.

David, laughing, asked if he might see a dove flying around the church, just as a dove had come to Jesus. Mrs Alexander asked the children what they thought about this – what did the Bible really say happened? Lisa pointed out that the story said 'God came to Jesus like a dove'. She didn't think a dove really came down. Mrs Alexander agreed with her. She taught the children that a dove is a well-known sign in religion, and usually means someone is close to God, and is feeling peaceful and content.

She was delighted when David offered an insight. Perhaps the dove at Jesus' baptism was something like the Archangel Gabriel in Muhammad's story? Mrs Alexander commented that in both Jesus' case and that of Muhammad something unusual and very important happened. Perhaps it could not be described in words, so 'picture language' had to be used. The lesson ended by the teacher passing around postcards of famous paintings of the baptism of Jesus. As the children discussed the pictures, Mrs Alexander reinforced the points made during the lesson. As a follow-up session, she intended asking the children to draw their own pictures of Jesus' baptism, and to discuss them with each other and with her.

She felt satisfied that the children were beginning to understand the use of symbols and metaphors in both art and language. She fully appreciated though that the teaching achieved so far was very much a beginning which would need to be developed throughout the rest of their time in primary school, and beyond. She felt their Religious Education in the Early Years had set them off on an exciting journey of discovery and adventure.

A conversation: is God believable?

Some little time later, Mrs Alexander was circulating among the children who were engaged in craft activities. One child, Peter, asked her a question which led to an interesting conversation.

PETER My grandad says he doesn't believe in God, but my dad does.
TEACHER Did you ask your grandad why he doesn't believe in God, and your dad why he does?

PETER My grandad said it's just people's imagination.

TEACHER What did your dad say?

PETER He said 'Look at everything in our world! How could our bodies be just an accident? They are too clever! Look at the beauty of a flower! How could that just be an accident?'

TEACHER Yes. People who follow the Sikh religion say God is to their lives just as the scent is to the flower. What do you think they might mean?

PETER I'm not sure. Do they mean God has a lovely smell?

TEACHER Well, the thing is this. You cannot separate a flower from its scent – it is part of it, and important to it. I think the Sikh might mean God is part of their lives and cannot be taken away. Can you think of any other examples?

[David and Sharon had been listening to this conversation and had something to contribute.]

DAVID I think I've had an idea! It's like saying God is to a person as whiteness is to milk!

PETER Yes! Or as colours are to the rainbow! Or as water is to wetness! I see what you mean.

SHARON My mum is always saying my knees are dirty. Maybe God is to people as my dirty knees are to me!

TEACHER [laughing] Something like that! In other words, whether people can believe in God depends on how they understand what 'God' means. Peter, why don't you discuss these ideas further with your grandad and your dad tonight?

PETER Yes, I will.

Assessment, recording and reporting

At the end of each lesson, Mrs Alexander made notes about the children's work, any insights they might have expressed, and samples of work produced to illustrate the points she had made. In addition, she devised the self-assessment form which is reproduced in Box 10.9 as she believed that as they approached the end of Key Stage 1, children should be encouraged to express and record their perceptions of work in Religious Education.

Box 10.9 Self-assessment sheet, Year 2: Religious Education

Name .... Date ....

Lesson ....

1   Did you enjoy your lesson? Why/why not?

. . . .

2   Did you say anything to the teacher about the lesson? If so, what?

. . . .

3   What feelings did the lesson give you?

. . . .

4   Did you learn any new words during the lesson?

. . . .

5   In your own words, write on these lines what you think the
     lesson was about:

. . . .

. . . .

TEACHER'S COMMENTS:

11

COLLECTIVE WORSHIP
IN EDUCATION

Introduction

The legal requirements surrounding Collective Worship in county schools are described in Appendix A. It is the purpose of this chapter to discuss the real situation in schools, where teachers have responsibility for organising a daily Collective Worship session. The focus is on how Collective Worship can be an educational activity, one that is part of the school's planned curriculum and which makes a positive contribution to the values of the community and the reflections and values of each child.

Education and Collective Worship

Voices are frequently heard protesting – from staffrooms, meetings and both private and public places – that it is impossible to conduct Collective Worship in the state school system because of the 'multicultural nature' of British society. How, the argument continues, can we force pupils to worship when many hold no belief in a God, whilst among the others are many children from a diversity of cultural and religious backgrounds? We can no longer, it seems, assume or expect religious faith or commitment. How is it possible to conduct 'multifaith' worship without offending people, particularly since pupils in schools constitute a 'forced congregation' of people, rather than one that has voluntarily chosen to participate in worship? According to this view, children depend upon their parents to exercise their right of withdrawal: without it, they are prisoners of the system.

How one views Collective Worship depends to a great extent upon how one understands the role of the school in society. To put it another way, it depends upon whether one sees the school as an educational institution, or one that is in the business of transferring skills, knowledge and attitudes considered to be beneficial for wider society.

It is the contention of the writer that schools are first and foremost concerned with the former – they exist to educate, that is, to help the individual pupil to develop whatever unique potential he or she might hold which will enable him/her to make a positive contribution to life generally. Collective Worship, as a central part of school life, offers a particularly interesting opportunity for developing this potential. This is because worship sessions are occasions when the individual can offer new insights, gained from either inside or outside of the classroom, to the wider school community for reflection. In addition, the work of the individual class can be shared with the school community, and hopefully on occasions other classes will wish to develop some of the ideas presented. Collective Worship, particularly because it usually brings together groups of children who otherwise work in other places throughout the building, offers a very important opportunity for examining the context of what has been learnt by drawing out its significance for the beliefs and values of the whole community. However, for many people there are several inter-related problems with school worship which arise from the use of the actual word 'worship'.

Definition of 'worship'

This particular activity – worship – refers to an activity or state of mind, a recollection or meditation during which people consciously relate to God. Therefore, it is impossible to separate 'God' from worship, since it is 'God' that is the focus of reflection and worship.

The question which arises from this is somewhat paradoxical. How can schools bring together people – both children and adults – who may not believe in the God who is to be the centre of the activity? Some have attempted to resolve the dilemma by arguing that 'worship' is really about 'valuing'. This, however, pleases no-one since religious people who wholeheartedly endorse the more traditional notions of worship see this as a 'compromise' position and an attempt to opt out of religion altogether, while those of a secular persuasion suspect that this is an underhand way of introducing religion: after all, why otherwise call the activity 'worship'?

What is needed is a way of retaining the religious definition of worship – since without it worship cannot take place – whilst at the same time offering people of little or no religious belief opportunities to participate.

Worship: levels of participation

The response of any group of worshippers to the 'worship' activity is certain to fall within at least two levels. The first is the *exploration* level, and here can be found the educational reason for including Collective Worship in the life of the school. To explore belief in God is an educational activity, since no-one can sensibly make up their mind about questions concerning God's existence without understanding what that means.

141

The second level is one of *adoration*, where believers have freedom to approach the God in which they believe freely and personally. It is unlikely that any participant will be operating at one level or another. Whilst for some it will be appropriate to respond at the explorational level, others are likely to engage with the materials on both levels, both meditating and reflecting and worshipping. Take the following children as examples of how individuals from quite diverse backgrounds can respond to worship sessions in ways that are undoubtedly educational.

- Melanie, who comes from a typically non-religious background, one where religion is never mentioned and where the word 'God' is only used as a swear-word.
- Aziz, from an Islamic background.
- Maria, who is from a Roman Catholic family.
- Saun, from a consciously agnostic/atheistic background where statements like 'we don't believe in God – that is just superstition' are characteristic.

Two of these children, Aziz and Maria, are likely to be able to respond at both the explorational and adorational levels, whilst for Melanie and Saun the explorational level is more likely to be appropriate.

In the context of the school, interpreted this way, worship sessions become 'assemblies which give opportunities for worship or finding out about worship'. Collective Worship, then, has much to do with bringing together the individuals who make up the community, providing chances for them to share their work and the insights which have arisen from it, and to encourage reflection on both. The collective activity becomes worship when children are invited to give thanks, in their own way, for the gift of life, which has enabled people to make progress.

The key word for understanding worship in the school setting could be 'opportunity'. Worship presents many different types of opportunities to those who participate, and as pointed out by Watson (1993, 166), it really does not matter whether the main impact is one of 'adoration rather than exploration', as long as pupils are encouraged to reflect in ever-increasing depth about the issues presented. It is for this reason that great sensitivity needs to be given to how, for example, worship sessions can be introduced in ways that are not offensive to people. Please refer to Box 11.1 for suggestions.

Particularly closely connected with the above is how Collective Worship sessions are organised, their content, and how planning can be undertaken to lessen the possibility of repetition and under-development. I shall deal with each of these issues in turn.

The presentation of worship

As the title 'Collective Worship' indicates, the assumption that the worshippers will come from a diversity of backgrounds, including those of no faith, underlies the whole conception of school worship. This is quite a different state of affairs from the ones to be found in organised religion, where the participants choose to worship. Unfortunately, however, it is a great temptation to transfer the language of the latter circumstances to the school scene, and to find oneself requesting pupils to 'Sing Hymn Number 45', to 'repeat after me the Lord's Prayer' or to put 'hands together, and eyes closed'.

As Harold Loukes explained over twenty years ago (quoted Watson, 1987, 189), pupils frequently resent what they deem to be 'orders' in Collective Worship, particularly if they do not necessarily share the beliefs of the leader:

GIRL: You have no right to make us pray.
HEAD: But I don't; nobody can make you pray.
GIRL: But you try to; you say 'Let us pray'.

Clearly, as pointed out by Watson, the girl felt 'got at' during such occasions, times when she saw assaults being made on her right to individual freedom of thought. As a boy pointed out to the writer not long afterwards, 'Why should I sing "All Things Bright and Beautiful" when I have just had a bad cold? Didn't God make the germs too? Why should I say thank you for them when they made me ill?'

There is a strong need to be ultra sensitive to the educative role of Collective Worship which respects the right of each pupil to respond individually. Therefore, it is wise to phrase requests such as those discussed above as invitations, rather than orders. The suggestion provided in Box 11.1 could prove helpful to teachers who have the responsibility of leading worship.

Box 11.1 Some useful phrases when leading Collective Worship

- This is a time of the day when each of us can do some thinking for ourselves. The story/ideas we are going to hear are very important to many people [*perhaps specify*]. Here is a chance to think about them for yourselves. Do they make sense to you? Why do you think many people find them important?
- Grown-ups have many different ideas about religions. Some don't believe in God at all, but for others it is the most important thing in their life and makes sense of all that happens to them. In

---

schools we learn about religion – about believing in God – so that we can make up our own mind. We can only do this sensibly if we know what we and other people are talking about. Do you believe in 'sentangles'? It would be silly to say 'yes' or 'no' if you don't know what 'sentangles' are, or is! We need to find out what 'God' means before we know if we can believe or not.

- Here is a chance to think in your own way about . . . .
- As you listen to the story, you might want to think about what it means to you.
- Join in the words of The Lord's Prayer if you wish, or perhaps you'd rather think about them silently, in your own way.
- Here is a piece of music called XXXXX. As you listen, you might like to think about the pictures it brings into your mind.
- Do you agree with the words of this prayer I am going to read?
- As you listen or sing the hymn for today, number 4, would you like to . . . .
- Let us have a minute of silence to think in our own way about something that is important either to you, or to someone you like.

The content of worship

The way in which Collective Worship sessions are planned mirrors their intention. If Collective Worship is to make (as it undoubtedly ought to do) an educational contribution to the life of the school and all who make up its community, the following objectives could prove useful as criteria against which to assess the content of sessions.

1 To offer pupils new ways of thinking about familiar phenomena and experiences, especially regarding how it might be wise to respond to them.
2 To provide opportunities for pupils to experience worship activities, for example, prayer and reflection on religious insights, so they can grow to appreciate worship as a natural activity for people.
3 To provide opportunities for pupils to celebrate, or worship, good things in life by encouraging the development of ever-increasing levels of thoughtfulness.

If worship is perceived in this way, its educational function will probably be clearer. Sessions will transcend the passing on of what is assumed to be knowledge and skills. Whilst insights and ideas will be offered to children, the underlying purpose of worship, as it would be in all teaching, is to attempt to stimulate pupils' curiosity about the natural world, the world of human creation, and insights into what could be appropriate responses to them, regarding both personal ethics and values generally.

In Box 11.2 are suggested criteria against which to assess the likelihood of pupils' interests and curiosity being both aroused and retained during worship (see also Box 12.7).

Box 11.2 Criteria for selection of Collective Worship materials

1   Does the material have inherent within it a sense of mystery, or unknown outcomes?
2   Does the material contain an insight, or insights, which have proved to be sustaining over long periods of time?
3   Are the children likely to be able to relate the material to their own experiences? (Note: historical or geographical distances are not necessarily important for them to be able to do so.)
4   Does the material offer a new way, or ways, of thinking about what is familiar?
5   Does the way in which it is proposed to present the materials offer the children scope for personal reflection, perhaps during moments of silence?
6   Does the material encourage the children to move on from simplistic levels of thought (for example, concerning the possible meanings of miracles), to ones that are deeper?
7   Does the material encourage the children to question, and possibly take on board, new ideas for testing and possible adoption?

The organisation of worship

Primarily the organisation of Collective Worship, in a state school, rests with the Governing Body and the Head Teacher. One is entitled to assume that Heads will include the staff in discussions of organisation. Under current legislation, an Act of Worship must be provided for each child on each school day (unless the child's parents exercise the right of withdrawal – see Appendix A). The legislation of 1988 made several important changes to previous requirements and this has altered considerably what actually happens in schools, for example:

1   Unlike the 1944 Education Act, the school day is no longer required to begin with an Act of Collective Worship.
2   There can be more than one Act of Collective Worship in the school day.

Whilst these new requirements undoubtedly have done much to change the physical difficulties facing large schools in the comprehensive sector, they have also ushered into the primary schools much greater flexibility, for classes are now entitled to conduct their worship individually or in groupings which could vary from one school day to the other. Additionally, worship can take place at any time during the school day. The advantages of such flexibility are obvious, including perhaps the freedom teachers now have to organise pupils in groups that allow the content of worship to be pitched appropriately.

In Box 11.3 is set out a pattern for the organisation of Collective Worship which is commonly found in primary schools.

Box 11.3 Weekly timetable for primary school Collective Worship

Monday	Key Stage 1 – 10.00 Main Hall. Taken by Mr Smith, Dep. Head. Key Stage 2 – 9.30 Main Hall. Taken by Mrs Jones, Head.
Tuesday	Key Stages 1 and 2 together – 10.10 Main Hall. Taken by Mrs Jones, Head.
Wednesday	Classes R, Year 1, Year 2, Year 3 and Year 4 – 10.10, Main Hall. Taken by Miss Jackson, Head of Lower School. Classes 5 and 6 together in Room 5. Taken alternatively by class teachers.
Thursday	Whole school – 10.00 Main Hall. Class Collective Worship. (School, from Middle Infants upwards, are on a rota for organising worship sessions.) Parents invited.
Friday	Key Stage 1 – 10.00 Main Hall. Taken by Miss Jackson, Lower School Head. Key Stage 2 – 3.10 Main Hall. Taken by Mrs Jones. End of Week Collective Worship

Note: Throughout the year, this plan could be varied to allow, for example, Harvest or other Festival celebrations to be held elsewhere.

Of particular note is the need for teachers to remember where, and at what time, to be ready for Collective Worship! In addition, schools usually have their own systems for letting classes know which hymn books will be required for individual sessions.

There exist other considerations which, whilst perhaps seemingly trivial to teachers, are of great importance to children, as enquiries among them have revealed to the writer. Pupils regularly express concern about:

1   Having to sit on the floor during worship, thus covering their clothes with dust.
2   Having to sit cross-legged – children regularly complain of being too stiff to walk!
3   Being (a) unable to see pictures/diagrams shown during worship or (b) being unable to hear people reading. Both are extremely frustrating.

Whilst the above three points are of great importance, especially regarding respect for pupils, there is another complaint which is often heard from past pupils, which relates to another aspect of Collective Worship, that is, the way in which it is presented.

Planning worship

Planning worship sessions in advance is much to be recommended. Why this is so is not difficult to understand, and yet schools that actually do plan and record what happens in worship seem to be very rare indeed. The virtues of doing so include the following.

1   Records of worship sessions are a valuable repository of ideas.
2   Recording of worship sessions lessens the danger of repetition. As most primary school children will admit, repetition of material is a real turn-off! After several years of teaching, it can become incredibly difficult to recall precisely when certain narratives, prayers or film-strips were actually used.
3   If teachers have some idea of what will be presented to pupils in worship sessions they will be able to plan work which includes consideration of this context. In other words, planning can lessen the danger that what goes on in Collective Worship will be isolated from work in other areas of the curriculum.
4   The content of Collective Worship can be closely linked with work done in the Literacy Hour.
5   Particularly since the 'class assembly' has become a regular feature of the school week, when the worship is actually taken by children, it is important that teachers should work together in order to provide some continuity, or development of ideas. Otherwise, the content of Collective Worship can easily become superficial.
6   Collective Worship does much to reflect the values and ethos of the

school community. Records kept are an invaluable source of information for interested parties, for example, parents, OFSTED Inspectors or any other person with a particular interest in the proceedings.

It is suggested that teachers might find it useful to plan worship on a half-termly basis. This is a realistic timescale, as it looks ahead over a manageable period of time. It is important that teachers should agree on a general theme for the sessions, because as pointed out above, this will encourage continuity and discourage superficiality. It could be helpful for schools if a Collective Worship Record Book was kept, and made available throughout the working week so that teaching staff who would be leading or organising sessions could record what took place.

Suitable themes for Early Years Collective Worship sessions are provided in Box 11.4.

Box 11.4 Themes for Early Years Collective Worship sessions

Term One (weeks 1–7)   Fruits of the Harvest and New Beginnings
       (weeks 8–13)   Light and Darkness

Term Two (weeks 1–7)   Animals and Birds
       (weeks 8–12)   Springtime and Rebirth

Term Three (weeks 1–7)   Gardens

Term Four (weeks 8–12)   Journeys of Adventure

Box 11.5 shows how the weekly plan and assessment of the sessions carried out by the school could be recorded. It might be useful to reflect on possible pupil responses to the following sessions.

Box 11.5 Timetable for Early Years Collective Worship: harvest theme

Date: Week commencing Monday 12 September
Theme: Fruits of the Harvest

Monday   Joint session: all classes, Reception to Year 6. Listening to music: 'Four Seasons', Vivaldi. 'Autumn'. Mr Smith spoke to the children about different types of seeds, and showed them examples – poppy seed cases, dandelion

---

clocks, burdock, sycamore seeds, horse-chestnuts and goose-grass. Children tried dispersing the seed themselves. Mr Smith told a story about a conker fight, and two children from Year 2 gave a demonstration.

Children were invited to sing the hymn 'Autumn Days' and to think about a prayer which was written and read by Colin Thompson from Year 5. The prayer was about the wonders of the natural world.

Tuesday   Early Years Department: parents were invited to the Harvest Festival Service. The children's work was on display (e.g. drawings of fruit, flowers and vegetables). A display of harvest produce was laid out on a table. Parents had arranged this, with the help of children from Years 1 and 2. Produce had been brought by teachers, children and parents.

A religious leader from the Islamic community spoke for about five minutes on fruit and seeds. He suggested to the children they were a bit like seed, because they had a lot of growing to do! He selected examples of the fruit, and spoke to the children on how good it always was to see attractive fruit, because of its usefulness and the pleasure it gave people. We should do our best to be attractive, too!

Reception children chanted a couple of verses called 'Juicy Grapes', and a few children from Years 1 and 2 said a few sentences about the work that was on display. Mr Hussein then suggested that everyone should close their eyes and either give thanks to God for the harvest in their own way or perhaps think about harvest and any questions they would like to ask about them, perhaps in the classroom later.

The service finished with Gary Newton playing the chorus of 'We Plough the Fields' on his recorder.

Wednesday   Mrs Jones told Years R, 1 and 2 about the Christian parable of the Drag Net. She illustrated her talk with pictures of fish, painted by Reception children. The session ended with a prayer reading, and a moment of silence when the children were invited to think about the Drag Net story in their own way. Listening to music: six children from Year 2 played 'sea music' on percussion instruments.

Thursday   Mr Williams played the piano – a piece he had composed himself which was called 'Rattling Seeds'. He then read the children the story of 'Jack and the Beanstalk', making the point we can never be certain how a seed would grow – it is a bit like us! The session ended with a prayer which made the suggestion that we have a better chance to grow well than seed because we can think for ourselves. Children left the hall as Mr Williams played his piece of music again.

Friday   Lisa Robson and Mark Jones from Reception planted hyacinth bulbs, helped by Marcus Adams, Aziz Abdul and Kerry James from Years 1 and 2. Mrs Jones told the other listening children what they were doing as they all looked on. She showed them pictures of hyacinths in full bloom, and commented that at Christmas their bulbs might look something like those. Mrs Jones then made the point that many people believe it is a miracle that such beautiful flowers could grow from such a dull-looking bulb. She told the story about the 'Ugly Ducking'. To end, Adam Jackson and Audrey Hanson from Year 2 invited the children to thank God for the world we live in during a few minutes of silence, or to think in their own way about bulbs, flowers and the wonders of the natural world.

12

IN-SERVICE ACTIVITIES FOR STAFF DEVELOPMENT DAYS

Introduction

Teachers who have responsibility for organising staff development sessions should find the activities suggested in this chapter helpful. They have been designed with the following objectives:

1   To help teachers clarify their own understanding of Religious Education in the school curriculum.
2   To provide criteria against which teachers can assess the value of the material selected for children's lessons in Religious Education. These criteria should also help in the identification of teaching aims and objectives.
3   To provide children with a means of assessing the validity of insights and ideas that are new to them.
4   To help teachers recognise what constitutes religious literacy and to assist them in making it an integral part of their teaching.

It is anticipated that the Religious Education Co-ordinator will adapt and add material to that presented, as he/she considers appropriate. In other words, it is hoped the examples provided will stimulate creative thinking into how lessons can be created, developed and assessed. The assessment procedures introduced are presented in two sections, one for teachers and the other for pupils. Material has been included under the subtitle of 'Background' in the hope it will be helpful for Co-ordinators with the task of leading the developing staff discussion.

Activity 1: thinking through religion

Objective: to help teachers clarify their own ideas concerning the purposes of Religious Education in the school curriculum.

Organisation

Divide the staff into groups of three or four people. Provide each teacher with a word-field (Box 12.1). Ask everyone to circle any of the words which they think could be relevant to Religious Education.

Procedures

- Ask the teachers to compare their responses with those of others in the group.
- Note any of the words which are thought to be controversial.
- Ask them to add any words that they think ought to be there, but which are not.

Box 12.1 Word-field: which describes religion?

faith   belief   non-factual   ideas   myth   indoctrination
conditioning   suspers ition   rules   authority   dogma   facts
opinion   ritual   non-scientific   fantasy   laws   magic   ethics
supernatural   outdated   wisdom

The Co-ordinator could encourage discussion by inviting the groups to contribute their ideas in a 'coming together' session. When drawing to a close the discussion initiated by the word-field, the Co-ordinator could then identify two key words – *facts* and *beliefs*, explaining that it is common for people to assume that some subjects, especially Science, are about the former, whilst arts subjects, such as Religions Education, is concerned with the latter.

It should then be pointed out that this is a false division, as is now recognised by most scientists and philosophers. The movement in thought which produced the fact–belief division originated in the Ancient World, but was developed particularly in Europe during the nineteenth century. It was believed experiments using instruments could eliminate the human mind from efforts to identify 'facts'. The movement is known as positivism.

However, it is now realised by many that what science is really doing is advancing theories, and theories should not be confused with facts! What scientists are agreed upon is this: every discovery leads to insights into the existence of huge areas of the unknown. Rather than arriving at 'facts', every finding points to greater depths of the unknown which requires more research and investigation!

None the less, positivism has had an immense influence on how people perceive arts subjects: religion is often thought to be only opinion, and therefore unreliable. This is why religion in the school curriculum is thought, by many, to be a controversial area.

The following boxes could be reproduced on acetate sheets for use with an overhead projector, to illustrate the above points.

Box 12.2 The story of Religious Education under positivist influence

Approaches from Early Times:	Nurture the young within Christianity. This was called *confessionalism*.
From roughly the 1960s:	Growing belief that religion was only opinion. It was therefore thought that the teaching of RE should be 'neutral'.
From roughly the 1970s:	Only 'facts' are valid for study! We need to make Religious Education respectable. Therefore teach the 'facts' of religion only. This was called *Phenomenology*.
From roughly the late 1980s:	Interest in the psychology of religion and belief that this should be trained. This led to the *experiential RE movement*.
Question:	**Where are we now?**

The Co-ordinator, during the presentation of these ideas, could develop each of the points with material drawn from the earlier chapters of this book, perhaps inviting colleagues to comment on their own experiences and perceptions of Religious Education, both as pupils, students and teachers.

The material contained in Box 12.3 could also be presented on an acetate sheet to identify some current thinking on Religious Education.

Box 12.3 The downfall of positivism

Positivist claims	• Only scientific 'provable' facts can be verified and shown to be 'true'
	• Everything else cannot be proven and therefore is mere 'opinion'
	• Religion too must be rejected on the same grounds

Counter-arguments	•	Positivism cannot be proven scientifically
	•	'Facts' are no more than theories
	•	'Theories' are human interpretations of experiences, as is religious thought
	•	Arts subjects, including religion, therefore have a value which must be recognised in all spheres, including school curricula

Supplementary material which could aid discussion is provided in Boxes 12.4 and 12.5

Box 12.4 Summary of past approaches to Religious Education

Confessionalism	'We nurture the young in the faith of our fore-fathers.'
Positivism	'Only "facts" are important.'
Panic in the RE camp	'How can we make RE "factual"?'
Notions of neutrality	'Keep your beliefs to yourself. After all, they are only opinions, not "facts".'
Phenomenology	'Now RE is secure; it is "factual".' Focus on buildings, ritual, the outward aspects of religions only and *not* beliefs.
Experiential RE	'Now we can train the emotions.'

The material contained in Box 12.5 raises objections to the opinions expressed in the above boxes.

Box 12.5 Objections to past approaches to Religious Education

Objection 1	Neutrality is not neutral: it carries its own values and produces its own distinctive effects.
Objection 2	The values hidden in 'neutrality' include scepticism and those found in positivism, i.e. the 'fact–belief' division.

Objection 3   The effects of efforts to be neutral are to foster indiffer-ence to religion, and even to initiate into secularism, which is itself a belief-system!

Objection 4   Why should scientific methodology be the only way of knowing?

Objection 5   Regarding experiential RE, it is dangerous for the teacher to assume pupils are all thinking according to psychological patterns: we are all individuals.

Contained in Box 12.6 are ideas for discussion with colleagues. The intention is to introduce an approach to Religious Education that is respect-ful of the teachings of religions and which values the wisdom contained in the scriptures of the great world religions. Therefore an approach to teach-ing Religions Education is outlined which aims at offering pupils the opportunity to evaluate this religious insight and wisdom against their own experiences of life.

Box 12.6 Characteristics of evaluative Religious Education

- Is concerned with religious truth claims.
- Aims to help pupils evaluate their experiences by including reli-gious teachings – among other insights – in their developing 'wisdom bank'.
- Explores the reasons for people having religious faith.
- Encourages literacy and clear thought about religious beliefs.

Activity 2: criteria for assessment

The objective of this activity is to suggest a means by which both teachers and pupils can assess the content of their lesson plans and the viability of what they have learnt.

Procedures

By way of introduction, Co-ordinators could introduce the idea of criteria, perhaps drawing upon the following ideas. It might be helpful to give each colleague a copy of the criteria (Box 12.7).

What are criteria?

The Co-ordinator could introduce colleagues to the criteria, drawing upon the following suggestions.

Criteria are queries which can be levelled at any new proposition in order to test its possible validity. They can be extremely helpful, especially on occasions when one feels particularly unsure of a proposition or when one is tempted to dismiss out of hand an insight which, in the longer term, could prove to be beneficial for society generally.

Of particular relevance to teachers is the potential of criteria for testing the value of the content of any particular series of lessons, and for identifying objectives and teaching aims. It is not necessarily helpful to use each criterion in every test: indeed, in some cases it would be inappropriate to attempt to do so. The criteria suggested are given in Box 12.7.

Box 12.7 Criteria for value assessment of lesson content

1	Strict logic	Are there paradoxes? If so, are they helpful?
2	Consensus	Would most people agree?
3	Explicability	Does it help explain something?
4	Workability	Is it likely to work in practice?
5	Comprehensiveness	Does it cover large areas of experience?
6	Beneficial consequences	Is it likely to be helpful?
7	Relevant authority	Would most time-tested authorities agree?
8	Positivity	Does it offer a way forward?
9	Sustainability	Does it offer support?
10	Openness	Is it open to new ideas and insights?

Applying the criteria

Pose the following problem to the teachers. A Year 2 teacher is wondering if it is worthwhile telling her children the story of Jesus' Nativity again. On searching through books, she comes upon a version which gives a new interpretation. However, the teacher is unsure of how reasonable an interpretation this happens to be. What is suggested is that the Nativity story could be calling for an improvement in the status of society's outcasts. The query to be tested against the criteria, therefore, is:

* *Could a reasonable interpretation of the Nativity narrative be a call for greater social consciousness towards those deemed to be social outcasts? Is there any evidence this has developed since the gospel was written?*

Colleagues, working in pairs, could then be given about twenty minutes to apply the criteria to the above query. When this task has been completed, the Co-ordinator could discuss the results of the teachers' work, comparing it with Box 12.8 which could be displayed on acetate with an overhead projector.

Box 12.8 Teachers' responses to criteria

1	Does it have paradoxes?	Yes. God as a baby; being born in a stable; shepherds (outcasts) hearing the announcement of the birth of the Messiah first. This introduces controversy from the beginning.
2	Would most people agree?	Yes, although it is something constantly debated.
3	Does it explain something?	Yes. It moves the Nativity narrative beyond a pretty story to one that challenges 'social assumptions'.
4	Is it likely to work in practice?	Yes. Improvements have been made during the past centuries. In many parts of the world there is greater concern for the poor.
5	Does it cover large areas of experience?	Yes – internationally and throughout all periods of time.
6	Could it be helpful?	Yes – society would be, and in many instances has, improved significantly.
7	Would most authorities agree?	Most authorities in areas where it has been implemented have seen vast improvements on past practices.
8	Does it offer a way forward?	Most definitely.
9	Does it offer support?	Most definitely.
10	Is it open to new ideas and insights?	Without a doubt.

Children in Year 2 apply some criteria to lessons

Working in pairs, the teachers could then discuss which of the criteria could be used by Year 2 children in order to assess the point being made in this interpretation of the Nativity story. It could be suggested that the children might only be able to work with three of four of the criteria. Teachers should feel free to re-word the criteria as appropriate for their children.

In Box 12.9 are the results of children's evaluations carried out with a Year 2 class, which could be useful as a comparison with the ideas of the teachers.

Box 12.9 Year 2 children apply the criteria to the Nativity narrative

1	Does the idea ring true?	'You would have thought the angels would have gone to the King, not scruffy old shepherds.' Therefore the interpretation seems reasonable.
2	Does it help us understand?	'The story might have been saying something like "poor people matter, too".'
3	Is it likely to work?	'We don't laugh at shepherds and binmen now.'
4	Could it help?	'It might help us to be kinder to people.'

Having studied the above material, teachers might find it useful to assess how they might apply the criteria to other lesson materials themselves, and to select criteria for the use of some children. Examples of lessons could be:

- The resurrection of Jesus of Nazareth, and how it has given hope to generations of people (see Box A1 in Appendix D).
- The story of Prince Siddhartha (the Buddha) has been found helpful by generations of people seeking for ways of making sense of life (see Boxes 10.4 and A2 in Appendix E).
- Celebration of the Hindu festival of Holi encourages positive approaches to life (see Box A4 in Appendix E).
- Teaching the story of Hanukkah reinforces understanding of the significance of light as a symbol of God in world religions (see Boxes 9.3 and 9.4).

Finally, teachers might be interested in applying the criteria to lessons of their own choosing, and selecting and re-wording (if necessary) some of the criteria for use by their pupils.

Activity 3: Religious Education and literacy

The objective here is to help teachers plan Religious Education lessons that contribute to the development of literacy.

Background

Because religion is concerned with faith in God, and truth claims, whichever tradition is being studied, it is frequently the case that communication of the resulting insights and ideas cannot be communicated in direct, straightforward language. Even if this was felt to be possible, the use of metaphor still has the potential to engage understanding at much deeper levels.

The following suggestions for introducing teachers to metaphor should be useful in that they guard against notions that metaphor can be adequately dealt with in a single lesson. They should encourage appreciation of the insight that metaphor works by suggesting similarities between the familiar and the new, or by illuminating an insight in the light of what is well-known.

Procedure

Divide the teachers into groups of three or four. They could then be asked to highlight what they select as being metaphors in the phrase field given in Box 12.10.

Box 12.10 Phrase-field: which are metaphors?

- Her face is a red rose
- The Lord is my Shepherd

- An army marches on its stomach
- Life is a journey
- Could I please have some water?
- Light was coming as he laid the book down

- She travelled first class
- Our Father, which art in heaven
- Oh Death! Where is thy sting?
- Sit over there, please
- My love for him is a rock

- Her life was a fog

Teachers could then be asked to respond to the following:

- How did they recognise the metaphors?
- How do the metaphors work in deepening understanding?
- How did they attempt to interpret them?
- Can they create some metaphors of their own?

Misunderstanding and metaphor

A misunderstanding of a metaphor occurs when people argue something along the lines, 'Oh, it's not real, it's just a metaphor'. For example, 'God our father' is a metaphor of God's fatherhood. This could be an upsetting realisation for people, particularly if they have a faith in God but a misunderstanding of metaphor such as the one above. This is because God would seem to be 'just a metaphor'. Of course, the error lies in confusion – the concept of God is mistaken for a metaphor, whilst the metaphor is merely a way of expressing an insight into God – God is like a good father. However, God and the metaphor are quite separate.

The following activities could be helpful in dispelling this commonly found misunderstanding. It is important that it should be dispelled as it has the power to create even more serious misunderstandings in its wake.

Procedure

Ask the teachers to interpret the following metaphors, without explaining their source. They could be printed on an acetate sheet for use on the overhead projector.

A Christmas frost had come at midsummer; a white December storm had whirled over June; ice glazed the ripe apples, drifts crushed the blowing roses; on hayfield and cornfield lay a frozen shroud.

- How do we recognise the metaphors in the passage?
- How do we attempt to interpret them?
- What main points does the passage attempt to convey?
- How far are our past experiences important in interpreting the metaphors?
- Why would attempts to convey the emotion expressed through metaphors in 'straight language' be unlikely to communicate so deeply?

The Co-ordinator may find it helpful to note that the above passage comes from Charlotte Brontë's *Jane Eyre*. It describes Jane's desolation on finding that the man she loves and was to have married was already married to another.

The author uses metaphor to powerful effect – her emotional turmoil and devastation is compared with the promise of harvest becoming transformed into a winter scene. However, it should be noted that the use of metaphors to communicate the deep distress felt does not invalidate the distress! Her emotions were only too real, and the best way in which they could be shared with readers was through metaphor.

Activity 4: children and religious metaphors

The objective here is to help teachers identify metaphors which are regularly used in prayers, hymns, songs and stories, and to discuss how a study of them could form an area of work in the Literacy Hour.

Background

Children are regularly introduced to metaphors of a religious variety, particularly during Collective Worship. Hymns, prayers and religious narratives make constant use of them. However, work on metaphor which helps children interpret language beyond its obvious (surface level) meaning is rarely developed. The following activity is designed to help teachers plan lessons that will help children gradually develop an appreciation of metaphors and the ability to create their own in order to enrich their understanding and use of language.

Procedure

Provide the teachers with the hymn books, copies of prayers and the texts of stories of the type which are regularly used by the school. Working in pairs, for about forty-five minutes, ask the teachers to identify and interpret any metaphors used. In the case of each one, teachers could be asked to identify:

- How children are likely to interpret the metaphor.
- What misunderstandings could arise from their literal interpretations.
- Possible layers of meaning of the metaphor.
- How they could plan lessons that would help children to consider meanings beyond the surface levels of interpretation and produce sample lesson notes.

The staff could reconvene, and each pair could present to the rest of the group the metaphors they identified and how they responded to the above tasks, particularly sharing with colleagues their ideas for lesson materials and their development.

Activity 5: stories and values

The objective is to help teachers identify the values suggested to children in the varieties of literature which they introduce to them.

Background

Through literature, both religious and sacred, children are constantly introduced to a variety of values which play an immensely important role in values development and therefore the whole personality. For example, a six-year-old child once related how much he loved the fairy-tale of 'Jack and the Beanstalk'. This was because Jack, although constantly in trouble, was proved right at the end. This particular child, who was in dispute with adults constantly both in and out of school, had found the story helpful in formulating his perceptions of life! It is there-fore valuable for teachers if they have an opportunity to reflect on the literature they use with their children and the possible results in terms of values education.

Procedure

Suggest that the teachers might wish to work in small groups or individu-ally. Ask them to produce the texts of a few pieces of literature – either religious, secular or a selection of each. Their task is to analyse the litera-ture in depth in order to identify the values inherent in it, working for about an hour. The following points could help structure the activity:

- Why do you use this particular story/poem/miracle, etc.?
- Which values do you see as central to it?
- How have children reacted to it in the past? How would you account for this?
- Would you use it again and recommend it to colleagues?
- How do you see the literature contributing to pupils' spiritual, moral and social development, as required by the Education Reform Act, 1988?

At the end of the group/individual activity, the teachers could share with colleagues their findings and come to an agreement on which litera-ture they will base lessons in the coming four weeks or so, as an experimental trial. At a following session, the teachers could report back, perhaps providing samples of children's work, on progress made.

Activity 6: developing conversations with children

The objective is to help teachers respond to children's questions and statements in ways that both develop their religious understanding and contribute to their values development.

Background

As discussed earlier (pp. 45–52) there are two basic strands to the teaching of religion. The first is the planned lesson and the second, and perhaps more significant in the education of the child, is the way in which the teacher responds to 'ultimate questions', where children are likely to transcend the empirical realm by making metaphysical speculations in order to satisfy their curiosity and interest.

Procedure

Bearing in mind the material provided in Chapter 5, it is suggested the Co-ordinator could provide each group (of possibly three or four teachers) with a child's question and ask them to develop an appropriate response. The following points could be helpful in structuring their ideas.

1   What does the question reveal about the child's present levels of religious thinking?
2   What concepts would it be appropriate for me to develop?
3   Are there any sensitivities of which I should be aware?
4   How could I incorporate some of the child's thinking to work in the Literacy Hour?

Examples of questions which young children regularly ask are set out below. They could be printed on cards and distributed among each group.

- 'My cat died yesterday. Will it be on its way to heaven?' (Paul).
- 'If God made the world, who made God?' (Sharon).
- 'Why is Good Friday not called Bad Friday? (Melanie).
- 'I don't think there are any angels. Muhammad was just dreaming in the cave' (Patrick).
- 'It doesn't matter if I'm naughty because God always forgives you' (Lucy).
- 'I don't believe Jesus ever lived' (David).
- 'Last night my little sister told my grandma she was too old and it was time she went to Jesus' (Lisa).
- 'Why does God let wars happen? Why are there starving people?' (Lee).

The session could conclude by teachers discussing their ideas with the rest of the group. A valuable outcome could be for the teachers to identify the concepts that are characterised by the statements of how planned Religious Education lessons could contribute to their informed development.

Activity 7: children's God concepts

The objective is to help teachers recognise the problem of crude religious anthropomorphism.

Procedure

This activity is envisaged as being a development of other activities which deal with metaphor. Therefore, it would fit in well at the end of a 'metaphor session'.

Provide each group with copies of children's comments about God (Box 12.11). Give the teachers about forty-five minutes to an hour to read the comments and formulate their responses to the following:

1   What problems do you see in the comments made by the children?
2   How would you account for them?
3   What problems do they represent in children's growing understanding of religion?
4   How far do you think the comments represent conceptual development, and how far a repetition of adult responses to the children which are inadequate for helping them understand religion?
5   How would you, as a teacher,

    • develop conversations with the children which helped them move on in their thinking beyond crude anthropomorphism;
    • incorporate your teaching of Religious Education in the Literacy Hour?

6   Plan a couple of lessons, with objectives, which would seek to diversify children's conceptual understanding of the word 'God'.

When the groups reconvene, spokespersons for each could present the ideas of the group for consideration by colleagues.

Box 12.11 Children's comments about God

1   God is very kind to everyone in the world. You go to heaven when you die.

2　God is a good spirit up in the sky. Heaven is where the spirits go when they die.

3　God is our friend. Heaven is special.

4　God is your friend. He helps you when you are in trouble. He is good.

5　God lives in heaven. God listens to you praying and God is invisible. You can't see him.

6　God is invisible and he's not scared of anyone. He takes care of us. The animals are his friends.

7　God is grateful. Heaven is just a beautiful sky.

8　Heaven is a place where you go when you die. My mam's dad died. He is up there now.

9　We say our prayers to him and he takes care of us. Jesus died on a cross.

10　God loves everybody. He made everything. God is very clever. God is very kind. God created me and you. Heaven is where people go when they die if they are kind.

Activity 8: planning Collective Worship

The objective is to give teachers an opportunity to consider appropriate sentences for use in Collective Worship, and to identify levels at which participants at worship sessions are likely to make their own contribution.

Procedure

Have ready, for each group of three or four teachers, copies of Box 11.1, copies of two or three of the religious narratives from Appendices D or E, and a copy of Box 12.12. Give the teachers about an hour in which to work. They are asked to:

1　Select one of the narratives from those provided and plan an Act of Collective Worship which focuses around it.

2　Incorporate in the worship session, as appropriate, phrases drawn from Box 11.1, or include ones of their own.

3　Make suggestions at what levels children like those described in Box 12.12 could be expected to contribute to Collective Worship.

At the end of the hour reconvene; a spokesperson for each group could present their ideas to the staff and develop discussion.

Box 12.12 Children in Collective Worship: how will they respond?

1   Melanie comes from a typically non-religious background. Religion is never mentioned, and the word 'God' is only used as a swear-word. The family celebrates a commercialised Christmas, rather than a Christian one, and at Easter Melanie receives Easter eggs only because it is a tradition. It is unlikely that the family would attach to the custom any religious significance.

2   Aziz is a Muslim boy who is taught the faith of Islam in the Mosque on Saturdays. He can already, at the age of six, recite large portions of the Qu'rān. His parents are devout Muslims who worship regularly and celebrate the festivals in a truly religious style.

3   Maria belongs to a Roman Catholic family. She attends church regularly and is presently preparing for her first communion. Her parents belong to a church family group and are deeply involved with pastoral work in the Roman Catholic community.

4   Saun comes from a background which is scornful of religion. Comments such as 'We think religion is just superstition' or 'There is no such person as God; only science', are regularly made by both of his parents and siblings.

5   David and Angela belong to a Jehovah's Witness Family. On Saturdays they are often to be seen going around houses with their mother, selling copies of the church's literature. Their parents do not exercise their right of withdrawal under the terms of the Educational Reform Act (1988) as they do not want their children to appear to be 'different'.

13

RELIGIOUS EDUCATION
AND VALUES

Introduction

The purpose of this final chapter is to step back somewhat from the class-room and take a broad view of Religious Education and its responsibility for helping people, both pupils and adults, to think in an informed way about important values which are – or could be – at the very core of society.

Religion in society: the case of Britain

It is frequently asserted, in various ways, that 'Britain is now a multi-racial, post-Christian society'. However, underlying this type of statement are numerous assumptions and very few of them are historically accurate. What the assertion attempts to convey is a simplistic synopsis of what British society both *has been* and *has become*.

British society is a result of the past, which can be found in every aspect of living and it is not sensible to divide 'what has been' from 'what is now' in such definite terms. Moreover, what is meant by 'a Christian country'? Are there notions here of a society where people were 'once God-fearing, church attenders' who lived their lives according to Christian doctrine and ethics? When did the 'change' hinted at actually take place? The history of Britain provides very little evidence indeed that the population ever disci-plined itself this way, although throughout all ages there have been groups of people who have attempted to lead a religious life and persuade others to adopt similar values. The position today is not dissimilar.

Perhaps what we should be considering is not a 'post-Christian society' but a society which has developed over nearly two thousand years accord-ing to basically Christian values. The monarch is legally Head of the national church, viz. the Church of England. As in the past, the population comprises a diversity of people, including adherents of other world faiths and a majority who come from non-religious backgrounds, where religion is never mentioned and where 'God' is used as a swear-word. The latter group has existed since the earliest times and probably will always do so.

It is illuminating to reflect on the fact that most Muslim families living in Britain prefer to send their children to a voluntary church school, either Church of England or Roman Catholic, than to what they consider to be 'secular' schools where, for most pupils coming from non-religious backgrounds, religion is a closed book.

Religious Education is retained in the school curriculum because of the belief that the study of religion as a human experience has an important contribution to make towards the well-being of society, that is socially, morally, spiritually and culturally. From this broad overview of society and the schools within it, it is hoped that the role of Religious Education will be clarified: to help pupils consider ideas and insights which could enable them to become thoughtful, well-rounded and reflective individuals whose lives are firmly based within the wisdom of the human race as accumulated throughout centuries. This is because religious wisdom – whether or not one is a member of a faith community – has been found to be sustaining and helpful, especially in times of stress, both personally and corporately.

Varieties of experiences

The children whom we encounter in our classrooms are influenced by a great variety of factors, and their reflections on these experiences constitute the 'raw material' that will be worked upon individually and which will gradually, and progressively, create their personality. Students have often voiced the opinion that religion is a private matter, not something that can be taught. However, each individual makes his/her contribution to general society, and it is not possible to separate the results of religious faith – or lack of it – from the quality of the personal contribution made to the local or wider community.

Educators have always been aware that encouraging people to take on board wisdom, whether Christian or otherwise, is no easy task. As past experience continually demonstrates, sustained efforts in this direction usually become dogmatic and therefore alienating for all concerned, often leading to a loss of the wisdom that was at the heart of the religion in the first place. This is also true of, for example, secularism, which comprises a belief system with its own set of values at its very heart, as pointed out by Hulmes (1979). Even postmodernism, the latest movement in thought which, summarised briefly, asserts that we all make up our own reality, tell our own stories, is based on assertions with which not everyone can agree.

All pupils are constantly bombarded by values of many diverse kinds, whether they emanate from religions, materialism, secularism or postmodernism. It is not that a non-religious doctrine is value-free: it merely has a set of values that are different in that they do not have at their heart a belief in a God, which is supported by the religious truth claims set out earlier (Box 2.7). However, pupils will only be in a position to reflect on religion in an informed manner if they have been helped through their education to examine these religious truth claims for themselves, and the best place to make a beginning is with Early Years children.

Profile of achievement at end of Key Stage 1

If, during their Early Years of schooling, children can be helped to develop a deep interest in religious ideas, and to develop a fascination for interpreting layers of meaning in language and artistic imagery, teachers throughout the later years will be able really to educate in religion. This is because the problems caused by literalism will be reduced and the pupils themselves will have less to 'unlearn' (e.g. crude anthropomorphism) in order that their understanding of religion can move beyond simplistic levels.

Mistakes of the past have been concerned with under-estimations being made of Early Years children's potential for thinking in abstract terms (Petrovich, 1988, 1989), but also with flawed notions of how metaphor works in both thought and language. These misconceptions can be found to have originated during the period often entitled 'the Enlightenment'. As pointed out by Lakoff (1989), metaphors of various levels of subtlety can be found not only in poetic literature but also in the everyday speech of the workplace and home. This means that every child entering the Early Years phase of schooling has already formulated a very important foundation in language which teachers should find invaluable. In addition, most young children are enthusiastic about learning, as pointed out by Donaldson (1978). They are also curious and respond warmly to the mysterious, the exciting and any circumstances that have unknown outcomes. This combination of circumstances is an excellent foundation for studying religion.

Box 13.1 sets out suggestions of what children who have arrived at the end of Key Stage 1 could reasonably be expected to have achieved as a result of work done specifically during Religious Education and Collective Worship and also during the Literacy Hour.

Box 13.1 Profile of achievement: RE at the end of the Early Years

1 The child will show evidence of having begun to perceive that there are usually many levels of meaning in language.
2 The child will have begun to perceive that stories and narratives can be true in more than one sense, and that they are often based on past experiences with the purpose of teaching us something about life.

---

3   The child will have begun to understand the relationship aspects of the metaphor of God's fatherhood, and in addition is able to discuss other metaphors of God, for example, wind, breath, energy, electricity.
4   The child will have some informed understanding of the reasons underlying the major religious festivals celebrated in the community, for example, Christmas, Easter, Divali, Holi or Ramadan.
5   There will be evidence from the child's statements and questions that he/she has begun to reflect in depth on 'ultimate questions', and is motivated to discuss such concepts as fairness, forgiveness and sacrifice.

Religious Education and parents

Student teachers have frequently voiced their anxiety lest the lessons they plan in Religious Education could upset the parents. This view is usually aired when it is advocated that children are entitled to study the beliefs of religions, not only their outward aspects such as artefacts, buildings and rituals.

In response to this, the following are offered for reflection and, perhaps, consideration at staff meetings.

1   The worry of most parents from a non-Christian background is that their child will be initiated into agnosticism or materialism, rather than a religious faith.
2   Education is about introducing both tested and new insights for examination and consideration. Therefore, education in religion which fails to inform pupils about belief, and the reasons underlying the belief, is of dubious educational worth.
3   It is also true that education cannot be neutral: since we select materials for lessons, this indicates we intend to affect the pupils in some way; otherwise why bother teaching at all? The vast majority of parents are well aware of this, and support the work of the school.
4   Any classroom lesson which stimulates parents to discuss the content of what has been taught is an excellent development. Teachers cannot be in dialogue with parents about their children's education too frequently.
5   As pointed out by Hulmes (1979), avoiding a focus for Religious Education which has at its core religious beliefs, and refusing to divulge one's own opinion about a religious matter – or any other matter – does not achieve neutrality. Other values slip in, which frequently encourage indifference or, in the case of Religious Education, agnosticism which has its own set of beliefs and values.

Under the terms of the Educational Reform Act (1988), teachers have responsibility for contributing not only to the personality development of pupils, but also to 'society'. As hinted at above, what could be a better way than to encourage parents to become stimulated and excited by the work of the classroom, particularly perhaps Religious Education!

APPENDIX A

The legal context for Religious Education and Collective Worship

Religious Education occupies a unique position in the curriculum of schools in England and Wales. It is neither a core nor foundation subject of the National Curriculum, but is described as being part of the Basic Curriculum (Educational Reform Act, 1988). Until 1988, Religious Education (or Religious Instruction as it had been called for many decades) was the only compulsory subject on the school timetable. It is now the only subject from which parents and guardians have the right to withdraw their children. In a similar manner, all teachers may refrain from teaching religion to their pupils. Nevertheless, all children and their teachers are entitled to quality Religious Education as part of their education.

One example of the uniqueness of Religious Education is that the content of the teaching in England and Wales is determined at local level by Education Authorities who are legally required to set up a Standing Advisory Council for Religious Education (SACRE). This body includes four different groups to represent the local community:

1   Christian and other religious denominations reflecting the principal religious traditions in the area
2   The Church of England
3   Teachers
4   The Local Education Authority.

SACREs are, in effect, a type of watchdog, with responsibility for monitoring the quality of Religious Education delivered to pupils and for either producing its own Agreed Syllabus of Religious Education or for adopting one from another Local Education Authority. This Agreed Syllabus has a similar status to the various National Curriculum documents relating to the foundation subjects. It is stated in the Education Reform Act (1988) that the content of syllabuses must reflect the fact that the religious traditions in Great Britain are in the main Christian, whilst taking account of the teaching and practices of the other principal religions represented in Great

172

Britain (ERA 1988 s.8[3]). In Scotland, the content of Religious Education is determined at national level – it is part of the National Curriculum. The content of Religious Education can differ according to the type of school:

- For *county schools*, Religious Education must be in accordance with the locally agreed syllabus of the LEA in whose area they are situated;
- for *voluntary controlled schools*, the Religious Education offered is to be in accordance with the LEAs locally agreed syllabus;
- for *voluntary aided and special agreement schools*, the Religious Education offered is determined by the school Governors in accordance with the trust deed (or, where this provision is not made in the trust deed), in accordance with practice before the school became a voluntary school;
- for *grant-maintained schools*, which were formerly voluntary aided or special agreement schools or are newly established under Section 49 of the 1993 Act with provision for Religious Education, the Religious Education offered is to be determined by the Governors in accordance with the trust deed (or, where such provision for the subject is not made) in line with practice which existed before the school became grant-maintained.

Fuller details of these statutory requirements can be found in DFE Circular 1/94. Regarding Collective Worship, the Educational Reform Act (1988) states that all registered pupils attending a maintained school should take part in daily Collective Worship, although parents and teachers retain their right of withdrawal (ERA 1988: s.6[1]). These worship sessions are in addition to Religious Education. For county or equivalent grant-maintained schools, the content of worship is to be wholly or mainly of a broadly Christian character (ERA 1988 s.7[1]; ERA 1993 s.138[2]), although not distinctive of any particular Christian denomination (ERA 1988 s.7[2]; ERA 1993 s.138[3]). Full details of these requirements are available in DES Circular 1/94, and Chapter 10 discusses Collective Worship in detail.

APPENDIX B

Example of a Religious Education and Collective Worship policy document

The statements in this document have been constructed as a result of consultation involving both staff and the governing body of this school, and are subject to on-going review. Its implementation is the responsibility of the subject co-ordinator, who will consult with the Head Teacher.

1.00 *The role of RE and Collective Worship in personal development.*

1.01 We aim to develop in each child a growing awareness of the wisdom which is contained in the scriptures of the great world religions, and to encourage each child to assess for him/herself the usefulness of the wisdom as a yardstick against which personal experiences can be assessed and measured, irrespective of the religion from which it is drawn. This is how the teaching staff envisage Religious Education and Collective Worship making contributions to pupils' spiritual, moral cultural and mental development.

1.02 At the heart of Religious Education, as in every subject, is conceptual development. Development of adequate concepts of God is essential for understanding religions, and this is the main focus for teaching. It will be closely linked to work on levels of meaning in language, especially metaphor.

1.03 Children will be helped to formulate their perceptions of fairness, responsibility, forgiveness and the differences between right and wrong.

Regarding Collective Worship in particular, we recognise that children will participate at two basic levels, and perhaps at both. These levels are:

- the *level of exploration*, for children who are exploring ideas of God and the ethics and morality which result from the responsibility of faith;
- the *level of adoration*, for children who are accustomed to worship – for example, children from homes where Roman Catholicism is practised, or children who have decided for themselves that adoration is an appropriate response for their reflection.

2.00 *The aims and philosophy of Religious Education and Collective Worship.*

2.01 We recognise that it is possible to condition pupils through what is omitted from the curriculum just as much as through what it contains. A central aim of both Religious Education and Collective Worship, as in other subjects, is to introduce pupils to human insights which have been proven to be of benefit to people, especially in times of stress or crisis. Pupils will be encouraged constantly to evaluate these insights by using them critically to evaluate new personal experiences as they unfold.

2.02 We aim to teach Religious Education in such a way that it encourages a deepening of thought and the ability to make predictions of cause and effect, based on past experience.

3.00 *The legal context of Religious Education and Collective Worship.*

3.01 All schools are required by the Education Reform Act, 1988, to teach the Basic Curriculum, which includes both Religious Education and the National Curriculum.

3.02 All children are entitled to a daily Act of Collective Worship and regular Religious Education lessons in addition to the worship.

3.03 The syllabus for Religious Education in all county and controlled schools is written by the local Standing Advisory Council for Religious Education (SACRE). However, parents of children attending controlled schools may require that Religious Education for their own children be planned according to any trust deed in existence before the school became controlled (Education Act, 1944).

3.04 The Education Reform Act (1988) requires all Agreed Syllabuses of Religious Education to reflect the fact that the religious traditions in Great Britain are in the main Christian, whilst taking account of the other principal religious represented in Great Britain.

3.05 The Education Reform Act (1988) requires that Religious Education and Collective Worship are non-denominational.

3.06 Parents have the right to withdraw their children from Religious Education and from Collective Worship. Please consult the Head Teacher if you are considering exercising this right, or would like to discuss the matter further.

4.00 *Content.*

4.01 The Agreed Syllabus upon which the teaching of this school is based is XXX.

4.02 Religious Education will be taught mainly from the perspective of Christianity, as required under the terms of the Education Reform Act, 1988.

4.03 Another world religion which will be taught in the courses provided by the school is the Hindu faith, at Key Stage 1.

4.04 Work will familiarise children with teachings from the respective faith being studied, particularly encouraging them to evaluate their own ideas through the insights provided by story, myth, parable and artistic works, for example sculpture, painting, music and architecture.

4.05 Outside visits to places of worship are an integral part of the Religious Education programme, as are opportunities for children to speak with members of the respective faith community.

5.00 *Equal opportunity.*

5.01 All children have equal rights regarding Religious Education, irrespective of race, colour, gender, social background or apparent intellectual ability.

5.02 The beliefs and values of the families concerned will be afforded respect and consideration at all times.

6.00 *Planning.*

6.01 It is recommended that children should spend thirty-six hours each school year, at Key Stage 1, studying Religious Education.

6.02 All planning of Religious Education is done on a whole-school basis in order to facilitate adequate development, continuity, progression and coverage.

6.03 Whilst some Religious Education may be topic-based, it is not assumed that all will be taught in this way. Thus, free-standing Religious Education lessons will comprise a significant part of the work covered, whilst cross-curricular work, especially in language, will be developed also.

6.04 Termly and weekly forecasts should demonstrate how the aims and objectives drawn from the Agreed Syllabus of Religious Education will be addressed. Work in Religious Education will be planned ahead, in detail, either on a termly or half-termly basis, whilst more general, outline plans for the whole school over a period of two years will act as a guide.

6.05 Class teachers hold responsibility for providing adequate records for each child, showing both the work covered and the individual child's developing levels of understanding and motivation.

6.06 All teaching should be done in context: that is, stories from religions, for example, should not be taught in ways that distance them from the background against which they were originally written. This helps reduce the risks associated with distortion and stereotyping.

6.07 Work should be differentiated for different children, as appropriate.

6.08 In planning, teachers should look for cross-curricular themes that are relevant to the teaching of Religious Education, especially encouraging children to interpret language at increasing depths of meaning.

6.09 Different activities should be included in Religious Education. These include story, art work, drama, mime, discussion, poetry and group analysis of texts, where appropriate.

7.00 *Classroom management and organisation.*

7.01 Approaches to the teaching of Religious Education should be varied, including both class teaching and smaller groups working co-operatively, outside visits and addresses from outside speakers.

8.00 *Resources.*

8.01 Each member of staff has copies of the School Policy Document for Religious Education and Collective Worship and a copy of the Agreed Syllabus, together with the school scheme of work. Each teacher, working alone or in association with colleagues, whichever is deemed appropriate, will also possess detailed plans for his/her work with children.

8.02 Additional resources for the teaching of Religious Education are available in the staffroom 'Resources' section. These resources include books, videos, worksheets, tapes, artefacts and activity packs.

8.03 Religious artefacts should be treated at all times with the greatest respect and reverence, irrespective of which world faith they belong to.

8.04 The management of Religious Education and Collective Worship, and all resources for these areas of the curriculum, reside with the Religious Education Curriculum Co-ordinator and the Head Teacher.

9.00 *Assessment, recording and reporting.*

9.01 All work produced by children should be marked according to the school's marking policy.

9.02 Teachers' records should provide evidence of the quality of work produced by the children.

9.03 Samples of work from individual children should be included in individual profiles, dated and noted with the age of the child when the work was done.

9.04 Records of pupils' work and achievement should be passed to the next class teacher, or school, as appropriate.

9.05 The Religious Education Co-ordinator shall be responsible for evaluating and reporting to the Head Teacher the progress made by the school in respect of Religious Education.

9.06 The Head Teacher, or other member of the teaching staff who leads any Act of Collective Worship, will record that Act in the school's record book for Acts of Collective Worship.

10.00 *Professional development and training.*

10.01 All members of the teaching staff will be provided with opportunities for undergoing courses of training in the teaching of Religious Education. All such course attendance will be co-ordinated by the subject co-ordinator, according to the school development plan.

11.00 *Outside liaison.*

11.01 The Religious Education Co-ordinator shall consult with outside bodies, such as the local Church of England Diocese, SACRE, parents, or other bodies who have a legitimate interest in the delivery and quality of Religious Education in the school.

APPENDIX C

Public understanding of religion and the role of the teacher

The classroom teacher bears an enormous responsibility for helping pupils understand religion. Unfortunately, public opinion of religion tends to be influenced by movements in thinking which are in themselves conditioning and conducive to stereotyping. The stereotypes that are characteristic of general opinion may be found in the categories listed below, and often in combinations of them.

- Religion is thought to have been superseded by science.
- Religion is assumed to be characteristic of a past age, rather than the present.
- Religion is confused with superstition.
- Religion, particularly festivals within religions, are considered to be characteristic of childhood. This is particularly true of Christmas and Easter in the Christian traditions, where celebrations have become overwhelmingly exploited and motivated by commercial considerations, rather than religious ones.
- Religion is assumed to be a mere list of dogmatisms which have been formulated to keep the population in order.
- Rebellion – even of a passive nature – depends upon the assumptions of positivism for its justification. For example, if science has superseded religion, why should religious authorities continue to have influence over our lives? However, as shown in early chapters of the book, positivism itself has been superseded as a means of acquiring proof which is indisputable. Where does that leave religion?

The following points need to be stressed:

1   Education in religion focuses on helping pupils understand why religions advocate certain values in preference to others. The stress is on understanding. Religious Education is not about nurturing pupils within any particular belief system or religion.

179

2 Religion itself comprises records of human wisdom from earliest times which is applicable throughout all ages. This body of wisdom has been compiled as a result of experiences and deep, penetrating reflection on them. Pupils are entitled to become aware of these collections of wisdom, and to use them at any time in their lives when it would appear appropriate to do so. This includes reflection on whether there could be a God which is characterised by religious truth claims (see Box 2.7). In other words, religious wisdom (and the wisdom contained in other areas of study, for example literature, which have a similar function) can be used to calculate likelihoods – that is, they help people predict cause and effect, although not with complete accuracy, as conditions never repeat themselves exactly.

3 Rather than being something only appropriate for childhood, festivals are events in the religious calendar when people of that tradition – and possibly others interested – celebrate an insight which they have accepted as being true and informative for their own lives. Therefore, for example, the celebration of Christmas for Christians is not simply about giving presents and having parties: it is about the personification of God in the newly born baby, called Jesus of Nazareth. For Hindus, the Festival of Divali is not just a time for lighting lamps in homes and having parties. It is a time of celebration in the belief that the goddess Lakshmi will bring positive things to the lives of those who live a devout life. Therefore, festivals are not confined to a short period of a year: they are times when the particular focus of the believer is illuminated through offerings of thanksgiving and prayer to the appropriate deity.

4 Religion is not, therefore, involved with the superstition, authoritarianism or stories that are only appropriate for childhood. It is involved with insights into how reality happens to be, and types of human conduct and values which are likely to guard against catastrophes of one degree or another, whether these comprise minor emotional upsets or conditions that threaten life itself – for example diseases spread by promiscuity.

5 Unfortunately, codes of conduct or moralistic judgements which are conditioned cause people to lose touch with the reasons for their original formulation. Therefore, for many people even the words 'ethics' and 'morality' smack of repression. They are considered to be authoritarian measures to stop people enjoying themselves.

6 The focus for Religious Education which is advocated in this book, therefore, has at its heart the following beliefs.

- That there is a likelihood that there is a controlling, loving power working in and through creation which is manifested in diverse ways.

- That humans seem to have a natural tendency to be attracted to negative influences, as well as positive. Religion teaches that prayer, worship, reflection and other religious practices guard against serious errors of judgement which are likely to be damaging both personally and corporately.
- That Religious Education is about helping pupils understand, as appropriate for their experience, why religious insights have become formulated and to be invited to test their wisdom for themselves. Whether pupils eventually develop a belief in God (in whichever form God is understood) is a personal matter. It is the role of the educator to ensure they have sound, informed grounds for their beliefs, whatever they may be. This involves conceptual development.

Just as the four rules of number are fundamental to understanding mathematics, so is the ability to interpret and create metaphors of God fundamental to understanding religion. However, as shown in early chapters of the book, there are many obstacles in the path for those who try to study metaphor, most of which have their roots deep in the intellectual development of the Western world.

The concepts of God held by any person are crucial for the quality of religious thinking which can develop, and for this reason it is advocated that most teaching in Religious Education throughout the primary school should have as its priority the development of concepts of God, closely linked with work in language – specifically metaphor.

APPENDIX D

The theological background to the Christian festivals of Christmas and Easter

Introduction

This appendix has been written at the request of a group of Muslim students who believe it would be helpful for teachers, like themselves, from a non-Christian background, to learn more about the Christian faith. Although practising Muslims, these student teachers pointed out that the celebrations carried out at both Christmas and Easter impinged upon their daily lives and neither should, nor could, be ignored. They were interested in finding out just why these two festivals in particular are important for Christian people.

The festival of Christmas

Advent: looking forward to Christmas (the coming of Christ)

The season of Advent, which means 'the coming', occupies the four weeks before Christmas and for Christian people is a time of preparation for the great festival of Christmas. Christians remember in particular the long journey made by Mary and Joseph from Nazareth to Bethlehem in order to obey the demands of the Romans that everyone should return to where they were born in order that a census could be carried out. The hardships of the journey are reflected upon whilst people pray and fast.

In many Christian churches candles are lit on the four Sundays before Advent, and special Advent decorations are hung, especially Advent wreaths which include four candles: one for each Sunday in Advent. One of these candles is lit on each of the Sundays up to Christmas. On the fourth Sunday, all four are ablaze. The use of Advent candles heightens the sense of anticipation. The darkness of the world symbolises life without the guidance of God, and the flame of the candle symbolises the hope given by the advent of Jesus of Nazareth.

Many Christians also exchange Advent calendars, where for each day in Advent there is a little door which ought not to be opened until that particular day has arrived. Behind each door is a special picture to do with the Christmas season, or even a tiny present or chocolate. The last picture of all depicts the Nativity of Jesus of Nazareth. The use of Advent calendars helps people to focus their minds on the religious significance of both Advent and Christmas.

The Nativity of Jesus of Nazareth

Discussion was developed concerning how the Nativity of Jesus of Nazareth could be developed with Year 2 children (see pp. 90–3). Additional information about the traditional site of the Nativity in Bethlehem is given below.

At Bethlehem there is a rocky hill which contains caves. Today this hill is part of the town, but in Roman times it was separate from the village. On this hill, according to tradition, a particular spot marks the exact place where Jesus was born. The Roman Emperor Constantine, at the request of his mother, Queen Helena, had a church built on this site, to which they both gave expensive gifts. Queen Helena visited the church for its opening service in about 327 CE whilst she was travelling to the eastern part of the empire. The remains of Constantine's church almost certainly lie under the present Church of the Nativity which is today a centre of pilgrimage for Christians from all over the world, especially at Christmas.

Christians believe that Jesus was not just an ordinary human-being but that he was God in human form. Even if the stories about the shepherds and the wise men, and the details about Bethlehem, the stable and manger, are regarded not as historically true but as parables, this still leaves the following statement which Christians believe to be historically true and which could account for the stories and other details being imagined:

- *God became a baby in humble circumstances in Palestine in the reign of Herod the Great.*

A special word is used to describe this event: *Incarnation*. This word comes from two Latin words meaning 'in' and 'flesh': 'in-carne'. It indicates the belief that Jesus was not just man, but also God – 'God-in-flesh'; the belief that in Jesus God 'spoke' to us and showed us His character by actually becoming a human being. Many people find it difficult to understand what God is like, so God gave them the closest possible visual aid – a human life, so that if people want to know what God is like, they can look at Jesus, Christians believe.

Do you think this is believable? Tertullian made an interesting comment on the truth of the Christian belief. He wrote 'It is certain because it is impossible'. Do you feel inclined to say something like 'I can't believe it because it is impossible'? Tertullian, however, was not a fool: he was a highly intelligent, well-educated, witty and practically minded person living in the African province of the Roman Empire about 200 CE. He was probably a lawyer, and not someone whom one could easily dismiss as a superstitious person, likely to be 'taken in' by fairy tales.

What could he have meant by this extraordinary statement? Probably that no-one could have made up so strange an event, one that is so much beyond anything we can understand and with our little minds, and which therefore is so hard to believe. We can say that people invented fairy stories, but one can reply that even small children soon realise that they are not meant to be historical. Christians do believe the Incarnation was historical, and to bring out the extraordinary nature of this claim as Christians see it, here is a quotation from some Christmas meditations by John Keble, an important Christian leader who lived in the nineteenth century.

> Think of him just born, yet having lasted for ever and ever . . . While he is everywhere, filling heaven and earth, yet he is limited and imprisoned within the size of a normal baby; he reaches not beyond the swaddling bands and the manger. He weeps for cold, pain and hunger all the while that he is providing for the wants of the whole world. He is all-wise, nothing is hidden from him; yet behold! he is content to be as other infants, ignorant and simple, to grow slowly in wisdom and stature. He is owner and possessor and Lord of all things, yet there is no room for him in the Inn. He is King of the whole world, yet he submits to be ordered and taxed by Caesar.

Do you think Christians are correct in their belief? How can one decide?

The Feast of the Epiphany

Christmas celebrations officially end on 6 January, although Christians celebrate the life and work of Jesus of Nazareth throughout the year. The date of 6 January is significant for two main reasons. First, it is the last day of Christmas (Twelfth Night), when decorations should be removed. Second, it is The Feast of the Epiphany, when Christians remember the visit made to the young Jesus by 'Wise Men from the East', who followed a bright star in their search for the young Jesus. Although this visit is often shown being made to the manger, in the stable, the gospel of Matthew (which is the only Biblical account of the Wise Men's visit) states they saw the young child and his mother 'in the house', and laid before him gifts of gold, frankincense and myrrh.

What might this story of the visit of the Wise Men mean? There are several possibilities, and teachers might be able to think of ones in addition to those suggested below.

1　The story could be historically true, as it was recorded by Matthew.
2　The story could have been imagined in order to make some important
　　points about Jesus, both his coming into the world and his later life, for
　　example:

- He brought hope (symbolised by the bright star followed by the
  Wise Men) to people, especially those who were outcasts in society.
- His message was for all people, irrespective of which part of the
  world they came from.

The story, whether it is thought to be historically true or a parable, is
very important, especially for Christians, for at least two reasons:

1　It is vivid, interesting to listen to, and easy to visualise and
　　remember.
2　It expresses in fictional form, perhaps, something felt to be profoundly
　　true of reality itself.

The Festival of Easter

Lent

Lent is the name given to the forty days before Easter when Christians
often fast and meditate, anticipating the death of Jesus of Nazareth by crucifixion under the Roman rulers of Palestine in the first century CE.

Holy Week

The last full week before Easter is called Holy Week, and it is a very important time for Christians because they remember and meditate on the last
week in the life of Jesus of Nazareth. Holy Week begins on *Palm Sunday*
(the last Sunday before Easter Sunday), when Jesus' last journey to
Jerusalem is remembered. The Bible gives an account of the journey, when
he rode a donkey through crowds of cheering people who threw branches
of palm on the road for the donkey to walk on (palm is a sign of victory,
and a donkey a sign of humility). Christians remember the events of Palm
Sunday when they receive, at many churches, a palm leaf folded into the
shape of a cross.

The Thursday of Holy Week is called *Maundy Thursday* (the word
'Maundy' means 'service', specifically the action of Jesus when he humbly
washed the feet of his disciples). The important event of Maundy
Thursday is the Last Supper – the last meal Jesus of Nazareth shared with
his disciples before being arrested in the Garden of Gethsamene by the
Chief Priests.

After interrogation, Jesus was handed over to the Roman Governor, Pontius Pilate, for examination. On *Good Friday* he was scourged by the soldiers and interviewed by Pilate before being delivered to be crucified on Golgotha ('the place of a skull') outside the walls of Jerusalem. He died during the afternoon, when darkness is stated, in the Bible, to have come early.

Easter

Easter Sunday is the Sunday following Good Friday and Easter Saturday. For Christians it is perhaps the most important day of the year, because it is when they celebrate the resurrection from the dead of Jesus of Nazareth. In Box A1 is an account of that first Easter morning, as it could be related to Early Years children.

Box A1 Narrative: 'The Story of Jesus' Resurrection'

It was still quite dark when Mary Magdalene, one of Jesus' friends, cried bitterly in the garden, near to where the body of Jesus had been laid to rest in a rocky cave. Mary was crying because, not only was she so sad at Jesus' death, but now she could not even find his body to rub on it the precious ointments and spices which she had brought. She couldn't even do that little thing for Jesus now: the body had gone from the cave!

In misery, Mary walked in the garden. She hardly noticed the first few streaks of light which were beginning to appear in the dark sky, and nearly bumped into a man who was standing behind her in the shadows. She felt sure he must be the gardener. 'Sir', Mary said to him. 'If you have taken him away, tell me where you have laid him so I can bring him back.' This was a silly thing to say because she could not have been able to carry the body all by herself and, anyway, those who had stolen the body would hardly give it back to a weeping woman! However, poor Mary was in such a state she just blurted it out.

The 'gardener' did not answer her question. He looked at her, and she gazed back, her eyes sore with so much crying. Then he simply said 'Mary', in exactly the way in which Jesus had pronounced her name. Mary gasped and looked again, wiping away her tears. The face was that of Jesus! Wild with joy, she rushed to him, threw herself on her knees and clasped his feet, sobbing in amazement. After a few moments, Jesus said to her 'Don't cling to me, Mary, for I have not yet gone back to the Father. But go to my brothers and tell them from me "I am going back to he who is my Father and your Father,

---

who is my God and your God".' So Mary, with a wonderful look now in her eyes, went and told the disciples that she had seen the Lord. As she moved through the garden, the first real rays of sunlight shone through the shadows.

The story of Easter is what Christians believe actually happened. People who are not Christians, however, think they are wrong. To try to find out who is more likely to be right is something like being a detective!

One clue is in the fact that there are people who call themselves Christians. There were no Christians when Jesus was alive as a Jew in the first century Palestine – he had friends and relatives and disciples like many other great leaders and teachers, but they did not worship him as God – indeed they were all Jews. As Jews, they believed there is One God who is the creator of the universe, the power behind everything that is. It would be very hard for Jews to believe that this God became a man – such a belief would be astounding and ridiculous for them. Yet, this is what Jesus' friends and disciples came to believe about him, because they were convinced he had risen from the dead and is alive forever. If we choose to think they were wrong, we have to explain how they came to believe it. We also have to explain how such a mistaken people – a very small group of unimportant people in a tiny part of the huge Roman Empire – could have started one of the strongest religions the world has ever seen, and in which millions of people today go on believing.

The death of Jesus of Nazareth is of major significance for Christians as many believe his death was a sacrifice – he died to pay the price of human sinfulness. This was the ultimate sacrifice which demolished the need for sacrifices to be made again.

The resurrection of Jesus is the core of Christian belief, for Christians believe that those who endeavour to lead a devout, Christian life will resurrect, after physical death, in the glory of God.

Notes for teachers

Christians remember Jesus' resurrection on Easter Sunday. A symbol of this is the giving of Easter eggs; just as Jesus' new life came from a rocky cave or tomb, so do new creatures hatch from their eggs. The egg is a sign of new life.

Both Christmas and Easter centre around the interplay of darkness and light, as shown below.

* Stars feature prominently in the narratives of Nativity and Epiphany, whether the light of 'angels' or 'the star' followed by the Wise Men.

- Darkness is said to have descended early on Good Friday, when Jesus died, but when Mary Magdalene discovered his resurrection, it was dawn on Easter Sunday, when light was returning to the dark earth.

The vivid symbols of light and darkness appear throughout the great World Religions, and provide a memorable focus for work with young children which is vivid and easily remembered.

APPENDIX E

Additional narratives for use with Early Years pupils

Box A2 Narrative: 'Prince Siddhartha, the Buddha, Part Two'

Prince Siddhartha had left his family and the royal palace far behind. He wanted time to be by himself, so that he could think very hard indeed about some important things that worried him:

1 Why are there such things as suffering, diseases and death – things that make people unhappy?
2 How can people lead a peaceful life, free from worry and suffering?

The Prince tried all kinds of things in order to find answers to these questions. First, he tried starving himself to make his mind really think, but he discovered he only made himself feel ill and weak. His mind couldn't think at all. Then he tried giving away all the things he owned, believing that if he didn't have them any longer, he wouldn't worry about them. This did not work either – his mind just wandered off on to other things which caused him concern.

Prince Siddhartha settled underneath a fig tree and forced his mind to think very, very hard indeed. He sat there deep in thought all day and all through the night. Some people passing by noticed him still sitting there in the moonlight. He had been there all day. They thought he might have turned into a statue because he was so still and quiet!

By morning, Prince Siddhartha had found answers to his questions. He now understood. This is what he had learned:

* All living things are born, die and are born again. The good or bad things people do make their lives either happy or sad. The choice is their own.

- People make themselves unhappy because they try to get impossible things.
- It is only by understanding you cannot have what is impossible that suffering ends.
- Loving other people and doing kind things will end suffering and bring peace.

The Prince now felt he was ready to go out into the world and teach. He became known as the Buddha, 'The Enlightened One', and today, thousands of years after his lifetime, he has followers called Buddhists all over the world.

Note for teachers A possible teaching focus is to help the children spot similarities in the spiritual lives of great religious leaders. Can they spot anything in the Temptations of Jesus of Nazareth, the Visions of Muhammad and the Birthday of Guru Nanak, for example, which are similar?

Box A3 Narrative: 'Joseph and His Brothers'

The well-known story of the great Jewish hero Joseph (Genesis 37, vv. 2–38) is available in many versions suitable for young children. It tells of the jealousy felt by his older brothers because he was their father's favourite, and how Joseph infuriated them by retelling various dreams which all indicated that one day they would bow down to him. They began to detest Joseph, and when he arrived at the place where they were looking after their flocks and herds, they seized him and threw him down a well, before selling him into slavery. Taking his robe of many colours, they dipped it in sheep's blood and took it before their father, Jacob, pretending the blood was Joseph's and that he had been eaten by wild animals.

However, Joseph was on his way to the slave markets of Egypt, where he was sold into the household of Potiphar, one of the Pharaoh's guards. After several adventures, Joseph found himself thrown into jail, where he met the Pharaoh's butler and baker, who were prisoners too. He successfully interpreted their dreams, and in due course was taken before the Pharaoh himself, and entreated to interpret *his* dreams. Joseph stated there was going to be a seven year period of good harvests, followed by seven years of famine, and he advised the Pharaoh to store grain in barns during the time of plenty, and then there would be food in abundance during the lean years.

Joseph was made the Pharaoh's vizier, and only the Pharaoh himself had more power than he. The time came for Joseph's brothers to go in search of food, and in due course they found themselves kneeling to the vizier, begging to be allowed to buy his grain.

Joseph did not reveal his identity to his brothers, but by a series of tricks endeavoured to discover if they had repented of their past conduct towards him. In due course, he admitted to them who he was really, and there was an emotional family reunion. The old father, Jacob, was brought to Egypt, and his sons were the founders of the Twelve Tribes of Israel.

Note for teachers The family relationships in the story of Joseph have much to offer children in today's world. Through studying his story, much insight can be gained into the dangers of boastfulness, jealousy and favouritism, and the importance of repentance and forgiveness.

Some Christians consider Jesus of Nazareth to be the second Joseph, or his mirror-image: just as Joseph was taken to Egypt as a slave, Jesus was taken to Egypt into safety from the wrath of Herod the Great.

Box A4 Narrative: 'The Hindu Festival of Holi: Prahlada the Prince'

Once, long ago in India, there lived a very vain King, who had one son, Prahlada. One day the King called all his advisers to him, as he had an important announcement to make. All the gods and goddesses had been abolished. Everyone had to bow down to him, the King, because he was the only god! His advisers made the announcement all over the land, and the King seated himself on his throne, waiting to be worshipped.

The first person to visit the King was his son, the Prince, Prahlada. As he saw the boy approach, the King pointed to the ground. 'I am the only god! Bow down and worship me!' he commanded.

But Prahlada laughed. 'No, you are not, father,' he said. 'I cannot worship you! I worship Vishnu, the great god!'

The King flew into a terrible rage. He shouted at the Prince, but no matter what terrible threats he made, Prahlada could not be forced to worship him. The Prince went to his rooms, and his father called his servants to him. 'Prepare a herd of elephants!' he screamed, in rage, 'and stake Prahlada to the ground! Then drive the elephants forward so he will be trampled to death under their mighty feet!'

Bowing low, the servants did as the King commanded. They dragged the amazed Prahlada out, and staked him to the ground with mighty chains. They then drove the elephants forward. They trumpeted as they charged – hundreds of them, trampling over poor Prahlada.

But what a surprise! When the servants ran to pick up his pieces, imagine their surprise to find Prahlada unharmed! 'Vishnu came to my aid,' he told them. 'I worship the greatest god, Vishnu!'

When the King heard that his son was still alive, he flew into a rage more terrible than the one before. He searched his mind for another plan that would rid him of his son. Again he called his servants to him.

'Gather together the most poisonous serpents in the world' he cried, 'and pile them into a deep pit. Throw Prahlada down into its darkest depths, and let the poison do its work!'

'Yes, your majesty', said the foolish servants, and did what the King ordered. A pit was filled with serpents, and the air was filled with their terrible hissing. Prahlada was thrown among them, the pit was sealed and left until morning.

Imagine the servants' surprise to find, in the morning, Prahlada fit and well, and sitting in the pit asking for his breakfast! They ran to the King, who fell into a rage even more terrible than the last. 'How can I rid myself of this son of mine?' he asked. 'How can I defeat the god Vishnu?' As he fumed around his apartments, his sister Holika called on her brother.

Now Holika was a witch, possessed of the most terrible evil power. The King told her of his problem: he couldn't kill Prahlada because the power of the god Vishnu seemed always to protect him.

'Leave it to me!' croaked Holika. 'I will get rid of my nephew. Just leave it to me!'

The witch commanded her servants to build a huge bonfire. They dragged up great tree trunks which nearly reached the sky, and the witch climbed on the top of the pyre, from where she could watch for her nephew, the Prince. At last she spied him coming.

'Prahlada, my dear nephew,' she cried, 'how good it is to see you!'

Prahlada looked up in surprise. 'Hello, there, Aunt Holika,' he cried. 'Whatever are you doing up there?'

'Climb up and see me,' came the reply. 'We could have a nice chat, you and I.'

The Prince quickly climbed up to where his aunt was perched on the summit of the pyre. She clutched him with her talons, and shrieked in wickedness. 'Now I have got you! You will die! You will die!'

Prahlada looked at her in amazement. 'Who, me?' he asked, trying not to laugh at his foolish aunt.

'You are about to die! Come flames! Come flames!' screamed the witch, hopping around on the tree trunks.

Prahlada saw enormous flames licking around, and noticed they were not touching his aunt. He cried, in a loud voice, 'Vishnu! Protect me! Vishnu! Protect me!'

In a trice, the flames turned from him, and blew straight at the witch. She screamed, 'I am burning! Oh! Oh! I am burning!', and died in the flames.

Vishnu had saved the good Prince, Prahlada. Evil had been defeated, and good had triumphed.

Note for teachers Holi is a springtime festival, when Hindu people celebrate the coming of the growing season with bonfires and parties. They rejoice that the darkness of winter is ended, and that the light of the growing season is upon them as they tell the old story of Prahlada.

Box A5 Narrative: 'Muhammad and the Camel that Cried'

In his earlier life, Muhammad had been a camel trader and knew these animals well. He had learned to love them and respect their great strength and endurance. Sometimes, when he was able, he loved to spend a little time in the gardens of Medina where the camel traders rested and had drinks. Usually these men remembered to tether their camels in the shade, out of the heat of the sun, but occasionally some of them forgot.

It was a particularly hot afternoon when Muhammad arrived at the gardens, and the first thing he heard was a terrible sobbing, cries that really touched his heart. No-one seemed to be taking much notice, but Muhammad could not feel happy when a creature was obviously in such distress. He went off among the bushes to find out what was wrong.

The cries were coming from an old, neglected camel, which was very near the end of its working life. Its owner had tied it up in the heat of the sun, without water, and the poor animal was in great distress. Going up to it, Muhammad fearlessly stroked the trembling beast and whispered softly to it, so as not to frighten it even more. At last, the camel became calm, and Muhammad asked around, to discover who could be its owner. At last he found him, quite a young man, sitting in the shade of a palm tree.

'You should be ashamed of yourself!' scolded Muhammad. 'God gives us animals and they work for us and ask for very little reward; yet you treat your poor old beast with great cruelty. We should protect them, not add to their troubles!'

The man moved his camel into the shade, and Muhammad reminded all present that whoever ill-treats animals is doing wrong in the eyes of God himself. Muhammad loved all animals and was concerned that they should always be treated well. He firmly believed that humans have a special responsibility to help animals, as they cannot speak for themselves.

Box A6 Narrative: 'The Adventures of Caedmon the Cowherd'

Caedmon was a young man who worked for monks in a monastery. His job was to look after the cows that lived on the monastery farm. He loved his work and enjoyed being out in the fields during the day or working in the farmyard, cleaning out the cowsheds and getting them ready for the cows when they came in for milking.

However, there was one thing that worried Caedmon a great deal. Sometimes he couldn't sleep because of it. After dinner, the monks and other people who worked in the monastery used to sit in a circle and sing songs to entertain the party of people. They had a harp and they would pass this instrument around the circle, everyone taking a turn to play and sing. Poor Caedmon always tried to slip away unseen into the shadows when his turn was getting near! The trouble was, he didn't believe he could either sing or play the harp well enough, and was worried everyone would laugh at him. He worried and worried about this and really didn't know what he should do. One day, he was certain, he would show himself up in front of all the others, and that he would feel really foolish.

Poor Caedmon! One night he tossed around on his bed of hay, sleeping very badly. He had a dream in which he seemed to be visited by an angel. He half-rose in bed and listened to the message in amazement. The angel told him he must now play the harp and sing. Caedmon replied that he didn't know what to sing about. The angel told him to sing about all the wonders of creation: the birds and animals, the trees and flowers. Caedmon began to feel excited and when he tried singing, next morning, he found it was really easy! He had a lovely voice, and the words flowed from his lips in beautiful melodies.

That evening, when he joined his friends after supper for the harp-playing and singing, he realised to his amazement that he was no longer afraid: in fact, he was really looking forward to his turn coming! After supper, the harp was passed to Caedmon. The men, he noticed, were giggling, as though they knew he had been afraid of taking his turn to entertain everyone. However, Caedmon fearlessly stood up among them, and played the harp beautifully. From his lips poured perfect tunes. He sang of the sun and of the flowers, of the deep forests and beasts who lived there. Never had the monks heard such singing before!

They were so astonished at Caedmon's rich gifts they invited him to be in charge of music in their monastery at Whitby, in Yorkshire. He worked there for many years, and the wonderful music he wrote became famous throughout the country.

Note for teachers The story of Caedmon was originally told in Bede's *History of the English Church and People.* There are many ways in which this story could be developed with children, for example, to help them talk about times when they themselves have lacked confidence and found that, after all, they need not have worried. It could also be useful to use when teaching about the symbolism of angels in religion (see pp. 71–3).

Box A7 Narrative: 'Henry of Coquet'

Henry of Coquet was born into a very rich family, in the country of Denmark. He had always been quiet and thoughtful, a young man who enjoyed reading the Bible and thinking about what it might mean. However, his peace was shattered when his family ordered him to marry a girl whom he did not love, and who did not love him. As he tossed and turned in bed, worrying about what he should do, he seemed to see himself rowing to an island and making himself a home there.

Henry felt sure this message had come to him from God, and he made his way to the monastery of Tynemouth, where he asked to see the Prior, the monk in charge of the monastery. He asked permission to make himself a home on Coquet Island, a few miles up the coast, a rocky little island owned by Tynemouth Priory. Permission was granted.

Henry built himself a little dwelling house on the island – a cell – and lived there alone. He was very harsh to himself, and the monks who visited him worried about him. He grew all his own food and in the last part of his life only ate three meals a week. He developed a very painful knee, which had an ulcer, but he continued to grow his food, limping around his garden with the assistance of a crutch.

In the winter of 1126/27 he was in terrible pain and couldn't move. He lay alone in his tiny cell, without light or heating and wouldn't allow anyone to see him. On 16 January 1127, a man heard angelic singing coming from the island, and Henry's bell could be heard ringing. A monk rowed to the island and found St Henry sitting holding the bell-rope in the light of a little candle. He had died, and the monk was certain his soul had returned to God. St Henry was buried at Tynemouth Priory in 1127.

Note for teachers   This is one of many stories about deeply religious people who gave up their riches for the freedom to lead a monastic life, away from the worries of the world. Another example worthy of study is that of St Francis of Assisi. An interesting focus for teaching is to encourage children to examine their values: Do they think God would approve of this strict way of life, or could they holy people like St Henry have been wrong? Did they simply go too far? How might they have thought about money in today's world? How far do the children value money? Are there other things more valuable? (See story of Midas, pp. 123–5).

Box A8 Narrative: 'Guru Nanak's Birthday'

Nanak had been deep in thought for many days. Early one morning, he made his way down to the lake to swim and refresh himself. He took with him a servant, to keep watch over his clothes whilst he was in the water.

The servant watched as his master waded out into the lake, going deeper and deeper. He noted how his strong brown arms cut into the water, and how quickly he reached the deepest parts of the lake. The man began to nod off in the heat of the sun, and when he awoke with a start, he looked around for his master. It was quite late in the day, because the sun was beginning to set. He looked around, expecting Nanak would have taken his clothes and returned to the village.

Imagine the man's horror to see the neat little pile of clothes was still by his side: there was no sign of Nanak! In despair, the man seized the clothes and clutching them beneath his arm he ran to the village. He gave the alarm: it looked as though Nanak had drowned. A crowd of men searched the shores of the lake, looking for Nanak's body, but no sign of it could be found.

However, when later the following day they made their way to the lakeside yet again, they were astonished to see Nanak suddenly appear above the waters of the lake! He swam ashore, hardly noticing he had been in the water for such a long time.

From that time on, Nanak devoted his life to teaching people about his new ideas, the ideas which had come to him when he had been in the waters of the lake. He had changed! He had experienced another birthday, and as a result he began a new religion, called the Sikh religion, which today has followers all over the world.

Note for teachers Guru Nanak, the founder of the Sikh faith, lived during the fifteenth century CE. The story of his conversion, called 'Guru Nanak's Birthday', could usefully be studied alongside 'The Temptations of Jesus of Nazareth' (p. 35) and the account of Muhammad's revelations (see Box 10.6).

REFERENCES

Ainsworth, D. (1983) 'Religion and the Intellectual Capacities of Young Children'. *Farmington Institute Discussion Paper No. 1*. Oxford: Farmington.

Allison, J. (1994) *Edward Elgar: Sacred Music*. Bridgend: Seren.

Ashton, E. (1992) 'The Junior School Child Developing the Concept of God'. In B. Watson (ed.) *Priorities in Religious Education*. London: Falmer, pp. 165–182.

Ashton, E. (1993a) 'Interpreting Children's Ideas: Creative Thought or Factual Belief? A New Look at Piaget's Theory of Childhood Artificialism as Related to Religious Education', *British Journal of Educational Studies*, vol. 41, no. 2, pp. 164–173.

Ashton, E. (1993b) 'Interpreting Images: An Investigation of the Problem of Literalism in Language Use and Religious Thinking', *British Journal of Educational Studies*, vol. 41, no. 4, pp. 381–392.

Ashton, E. (1994a) 'Metaphor in Context: an Examination of the Significance of Metaphor for Reflection and Communication', *Educational Studies*, vol. 20, no. 3, pp. 357–366.

Ashton, E. (1994b) *Celebrating Our Environment*. Crediton: Southgate Publishers.

Ashton, E. (1997a) 'Extending the Scope of Metaphor: an Examination of Definitions Old and New and Their Significance for Education', *Educational Studies*, vol. 23, no. 2, pp. 195–208.

Ashton, E. (1997b) 'Readiness for Discarding? An Examination of the Researches of Ronald Goldman Concerning Children's Religious Thinking', *Journal of Education and Christian Belief*, vol. 1, no. 2, pp. 127–144.

Ashton, E. (1997c) 'Readiness for Rejecting? A New Look at the Researches of Ronald Goldman into Childhood Religious Thinking', *Farmington Papers*, no. ES1. Oxford: Farmington.

Ashton, E., and B. Watson (1998) 'Values Education: a Fresh Look at Procedural Neutrality', *Educational Studies*, vol. 24, no. 2, pp. 183–193.

Bettelheim, B. (1991) *The Uses of Enchantment*. Harmondsworth: Penguin.

Blyton, E. (1965) *Tales of Long Ago and Yesterday*. London: Dean.

Caird, G.B. (1988) *The Language and Imagery of the Bible*. London: Duckworth.

Coles, R. (1992) *The Spiritual Life of Children*. London: HarperCollins.

Comte, A. (1969) 'The Nature of Positive Philosophy'. In J. Edwards and R.H. Popkin (eds) *Nineteenth Century Philosophers*. London: Macmillan.

Cooper, D.E. (1985) *Metaphor*. Oxford: Blackwell.

Curtis, S.J. (1953) *History of Education in Great Britain*. London: London Tutorial Press.

Day, D., and E. Ashton (1994) 'Subject Knowledge in the Early Years: The Case of Religious Education'. In C. Aubrey (ed.) *Subject Knowledge in the Early Years.* London: Falmer, pp. 178–187.

Deignan, A. (1995) *English Guides 7: Metaphor.* London: HarperCollins.

Depaepe, M. (1992) 'Experimental Research in Education, 1890–1940: Historical Processes behind the Development of a Discipline in Western Europe and the United States'. In M. Whitehead (ed.) *Aspects of Education*, no. 47, pp. 67–93.

Dewey, J. (1910) *How We Think.* London: Heath & Co.

Donaldson, M. (1978) *Children's Minds.* London: Fontana.

Ferguson, J. (1977) *War and Peace in the World's Religions.* London: Sheldon.

Fowler, J.W. (1976) *Stages of Faith: The Psychology of Human Development and The Quest for Meaning.* London: Harper-Row.

Friedlander, S. (1993) *Ninety-Nine Names of Allah.* New York: HarperCollins.

Gateshill, P., and J. Thompson (1995) *Religious Artefacts in the Classroom.* London: Hodder & Stoughton.

Goldman, R. (1964) *Children's Religious Thinking from Childhood to Adolescence.* London: Routledge & Kegan Paul.

Goldman, R. (1965) *Readiness for Religion.* London: Routledge & Kegan Paul.

Grahame, K. (1953) *The Wind in the Willows.* London: Methuen.

Guptara, P. (1998) 'Ethics across Cultures', *R.S.A. Journal*, no. 214, pp. 330–331.

Hawking, S. (1993) *A Brief History of Time.* London: Bantam Press.

Hay, D., J. Hammond, J. Moxon, B. Netto, K. Raban, G. Straugheir and C. Williams (1990) *RE Teaching: An Experiential Approach.* London: Oliver & Boyd.

Hull, J. (1986) 'Editorial', *British Journal of Religious Education*, Spring, pp. 60ff.

Hulmes, E. (1979) *Commitment and Neutrality in Religious Education.* London: Geoffrey Chapman.

Jung, C.G. (1940) *The Integration of the Personality.* London: Routledge & Kegan Paul.

Jung, C.G. (1941) *Modern Man in Search of a Soul.* London: Routledge & Kegan Paul.

Jung, C.G. (1978) *Man and His Symbols.* London: Picador.

Lakoff, G. (1989) 'The Contemporary Theory of Metaphor'. In A. Ortony (ed.) *Metaphor.* Cambridge: University of Cambridge Press.

Lakoff, G., and M. Johnson (1980) *Metaphors We Live By.* Chicago: University of Chicago Press.

Lovelock, J. (1991) *Gaia: The Practical Sciences of Planetary Medicine.* London: QPD.

Matthews, G. (1980) *Dialogues with Children.* London: Harvard University Press.

Matthews, G. (1984) *Philosophy with the Young Child.* London: Harvard University Press.

Matthews, G. (1994) *The Philosophy of Childhood.* London: Harvard University Press.

Minney, R.P. (1985) 'Why Are Pupils Bored with RE – The Ghost behind Piaget', *The British Journal of Educational Studies*, vol. XXXIII, pp. 250–261.

OFSTED (1994a) *Spiritual, Moral, Social and Cultural Development: a Discussion Paper.* London: OFSTED.

OFSTED (1994b) *Religious Education and Collective Worship, 1992/1993.* London: OFSTED.

OFSTED (1997) *The Impact of New Agreed Syllabuses on the Teaching and Learning of Religious Education.* London: OFSTED.

OFSTED (1998) *Standards in Primary Religious Education.* London: OFSTED.

Otto, R. (1958) *The Idea of the Holy*. Oxford: Oxford University Press.

Petrovich, O. (1988) 'Re-review: Ronald Goldman's "Religious Thinking from Childhood to Adolescence"'. *The Modern Churchman*, vol. 30, no. 2, pp. 44–49.

Petrovich, O. (1989) 'An Examination of Piaget's Theory of Childhood Artificialism'. Unpublished University of Oxford D.Phil. thesis.

Piaget, J. (1930) *The Child's Conception of Physical Causality*. London: Routledge and Kegan Paul.

Plowden, P. (1967) *Children and Their Primary Schools*. London: HMSO.

Soskice, J.M. (1989) *Metaphor and Religious Language*. Oxford: Clarendon.

Vidal, F. (1994) *Piaget before Piaget*. London: Harvard University Press.

Watson, B. (1987) *Education and Belief*. Oxford: Blackwell.

Watson, B. (1993) *The Effective Teaching of Religious Education*. London: Longman.

Watson, B., and E. Ashton (1995) *Education, Assumptions and Values*. London: Fulton.

Watson, B., and E. Ashton (1997) *Priorities: Grounds for Fresh Thinking in Education*. West Malvern: Moorhills Publishers.

Weaver, R.P. (ed.) (1982) *The World's Religions*. London: Lion.

Wilson, J. (1990) *A New Introduction to Moral Education*. London: Cassell.

INDEX